JULIUS NYERERE
HUMANIST, POLITICIAN, THINKER

JULIUS NYERERE
HUMANIST, POLITICIAN, THINKER

Translated from Russian by B. G. Petruk

Mkuki na Nyota Publishers
P. O. Box 4246
Dar es Salaam

First published by Benedictine Publications, Ndanda - Peramiho.
This edition is published by Mkuki na Nyota Publishers,
P. O. Box 4246, Dar es Salaam, Tanzania.
www.mkukinanyota.com

Editorial Board

Y.N. Vinokurov (Editor-in-Chief)
S.M. Shlyonskaya
Y.V. Dyachkova

This collection contains major papers delivered at the conference dedicated to the memory of Julius Nyerere, held in January 2000, at the Institute for African Studies of the Russian Academy of Sciences. Scholars, veterans of the diplomatic service and officials of Russian government bodies, having professional interests in Africa, attended the conference.

Cover Photography by Adarsh Nayar

ISBN 9987 - 417 - 51 - 5
ISBN-13: 978 - 9987 - 417 - 51 - 3

CONTENTS

Preface

v

PREFACE

The Institute for African Studies of the Russian Academy of Sciences held in January 2000 a scientific conference "Julius Nyerere: Humanist, Politician, Thinker", dedicated to the memory of an eminent African political figure, the first President of Tanzania who died on 14 October 1999. The conference was organized by the Institute's Centre for Tropical Africa Studies jointly with the Centre for Sociological and Political Studies.

In the opening address Director of the Institute, Corresponding member of the Russian Academy of Sciences Alexei Vassiliev noted that Julius Nyerere belonged to those few statesmen and political leaders of Africa whose names are becoming weightier with time, and whose meaningful contribution to the continent's history is still waiting for appropriate recognition. He called Nyerere "Mister Clean Hands" for his reputation as a transparent, honest man who served his people with selfless devotion.

Eva Lilian Nzaro, Extraordinary and Plenipotentiary Ambassador of the United Republic of Tanzania to the Russian Federation, noted in her address Mwalimu's (the Teacher), as Nyerere used to be respectfully named by fellow Tanzanians, high moral qualities, extraordinary modesty and outstanding intelligence. Speaking about the heritage, which Nyerere has left, Eva Lilian Nzaro emphasized, that first of all, it is a united Tanzania created from more than a hundred ethnic groups, which peacefully and with dignity live in a family of African peoples. The ambassador also highlighted Nyerere's great contribution to the development and inculcation of ideas of socialism in Africa, to the struggle against poverty and backwardness, as well as to the cause of African liberation from colonialism and racism.

Nikolai Kosukhin ranked Julius Nyerere on a par with such outstanding national leaders, as Mahatma Gandhi, Kwame Nkrumah and Gamal Abdel Nasser. The lecturer emphasized that at the epoch of the struggle of the African peoples for independence, Nyerere was not only a large political figure, the founder of the Tanganyika African National Union (TANU), subsequently Chama Cha Mapinduzi (CCM: Revolutionary Party), but also an uncommon philosopher-theorist. The main ideas of his works on African socialism are underlined in TANU's policy document "the Arusha Declaration" containing the plan for a socialist-oriented revolutionary-democratic transformation. Kosukhin also noted Nyerere's firm reliance on the necessity of unity and cooperation between African countries. He believed that the elimination of poverty and backwardness could become a reality only through cooperation with African states and other Third World countries.

The veterans of Russian a diplomatic service presented interesting recollections of their work in Tanzania, and personal meetings with Julius Nyerere.

Vyacheslav Ustinov, working from 1962 to 1966 as councillor at the Soviet Embassy and from 1969 to 1972 as the USSR ambassador to Tanzania, got acquainted with Nyerere, when the latter was Prime Minister of Tanganyika. Travelling about the country together with the Prime Minister, Ustinov was amazed to find in him a man of surprising sincere qualities, simple and modest. Ustinov underlined the outstanding role played by Nyerere in the integration of Tanzania and Zanzibar into the United Republic of Tanzania, his ability to lead the country along the path of progress without shocks and calamities.

Vladimir Aldoshin, a former counsellor of the USSR Embassy in Tanzania from 1974 to 1978, broached the same theme. In his opinion, Tanzania was at that time one of the centres of support for the national liberation movement in the southern Africa, and the role of Nyerere as the informal leader of the "Frontline States" could hardly be overestimated.

Vassili Solodovnikov, Corresponding member of the Russian Academy of Sciences, emphasized that the example of Nyerere, in the best way possible, proves that the African leaders came to socialism consciously and independently, rather than as a result of any choice, ostensibly imposed on them, judging from the publications of certain journalists and researchers. In his opinion, socialism as a concept of development has not left Africa in the irrevocable past, as capitalism is not capable of solving its problems.

Arkadi Glukhov, who was counsellor at the Soviet Embassy from 1968 to 1973, highlighted Nyerere's integrity of character and fidelity to principle. He cited as an example the event of August 1968, when Soviet troops went into Czechoslovakia. Despite friendly relations between Tanzania and the USSR, Nyerere denounced this act, and refused to support it.

Lyubov Prokopenko, Secretary of the RAS Academic Council for the Problems of Africa, acquainted the gathering with the modern political life of Tanzania, specifically with the activities of various political parties. She underscored that the most powerful and influential party in Tanzania is still CCM, originally founded by Julius Nyerere as TANU.

In his paper, Vladimir Ovchinnikov who met Nyerere on repeated occasions as a translator of the Swahili language, added a few deft touches to a portrait of Nyerere. He recollected Nyerere as a man of subtle intellect, who has made an important contribution to the intellectual development of his country, taking constant care of development and expansion of the Swahili language nation-wide. He personally had a perfect command of the language, and had even translated some works of Shakespeare into Swahili.

Deputy director of the Institute for African Studies, Vladimir Shubin, shared his recollections and impressions of meetings with Nyerere in 1997 and 1999, when the latter had already withdrawn from political activity, by retiring to his native village, but nevertheless, continued to take a lively interest in all major events occurring in the world and, certainly, in the life of his country, for the people of which he, would probably, for ever remain Mwalimu.

JULIUS KAMBARAGE NYERERE

Eva Lilian Nzaro

Mr. Chairman, Invited Guests, Ladies and Gentlemen, allow me to thank our gracious hosts, the Institute for African Studies, for making such hospitable arrangements for such a meeting, which is aimed at paying a special tribute to our former President and Father of Nation, the late Mwalimu Nyerere. I am glad that so many of you could come to this special function.

Let me begin by giving a brief historical biography of our dear departed leader.

Mwalimu Nyerere was born on 13th April 1922 at the small village of Butiama about 40 kilometres east of Musoma town on the shores of Lake Victoria in the northern part of Tanzania. He was the 26th child of Chief Burito's large family. At the age of 12, he was enrolled at Mwisenge Primary Boarding School in Musoma and showed extra-ordinary intelligence. He was then admitted at Tabora School, which was then an exclusive reserve for boys from the "royal" families of Tanganyika. It is at Tabora School, at an early stage of his life, that Mwalimu manifested his leadership qualities.

From Tabora, Mwalimu entered Makerere University College, then the pinnacle of Education in East Africa. Wile there, he was credited with being a very good and articulate orator who won praise and respect from fellow students. He graduated from Makerere in 1945 with a Diploma in Education and was posted to St. Mary's Secondary School in Tabora, as a teacher and that is where the word Mwalimu comes from.

After four years at St. Mary's, Mwalimu gained admission to Edinburgh University in Scotland, where he went to study for a Master of Arts degree, majoring in history, thus becoming the first Tanganyikan to graduate with a Masters degree. During this time, Mwalimu's vision of his future life, and that of his country, were even more refined.

His close contact with members of the Fabian Socialist Society almost certainly had great influence on his ideas which later on came to play a leading role in turning Mwalimu into a Socialist.

On his return home in 1952, Mwalimu was posted as a teacher at St. Francis College, then a missionary institution, a few kilometres southwest of Dar es Salaam. At this turning point, Mwalimu started to involve himself in politics. He played a very important role in the formation of the Tanganyika African National Union (TANU), a political party in 1954. A year later, he had to decide whether to become a politician or continue with his teaching at Pugu. Mwalimu chose the former. He was elected as the first President of TANU. From there onwards he led the fight for independence that finally succeeded in December 1961. Mwalimu forged a close working relationship with other leaders in African continent fighting for the independence of their respective countries. In this, he was a true Pan Africanist. Being a firm believer in Unity, he together with the late Naser of Egypt, the late Haile Selassie of Ethiopia, Kwame Nkrumah of Ghana and Ahmed Sèkou Tourè of Guinea, among others, founded the Organisation of African Unity (OAU) at a meeting in Addis Ababa in 1963.

In recognition of Mwalimu's efforts in the struggle against colonialism and racism, and his commitment to total liberation of the continent, the headquarters of the OAU Liberation Committee was based in Dar es Salaam.

In April 1964, Mwalimu was behind the union between Tanganyika and Zanzibar. Mwalimu, who ruled the country for a good twenty four years until 1985 when he stepped down, saying, "I cannot achieve in the next five or ten or whatever is left of my lifetime whatever I could not achieve in all these years that I ruled Tanzania." After stepping down as President and later as Party Chairman, he deeply involved himself in the running of the South-South Commission with its office in Geneva. He facilitated the Peace Talks in the war torn Burundi, and participated in the initial Peace Talks in the Great Lakes Region. Mwalimu vigorously championed the cause of developing countries' at meetings with the Bretton Woods institutions. His efforts have very much helped to convince the World Bank and the IMF to rethink their policies towards these countries.

Mr. Chairman, invited guests, Ladies and Gentlemen, having said that, let me now turn to the legacy left behind by our dear departed first President of Tanzania.

First and foremost, Mwalimu left behind a united nation; he left behind peace, dignity and solidarity among the citizens of Tanzania. He also left us a working constitutional system which allowed the peaceful transfer of state power.

Secondly, Mwalimu was a modest man. Poor as he was, he was a man of highest integrity, incorruptible and he did not mince his words. He called a spade a spade.

In the liberation struggle against colonialism and apartheid in southern Africa, Mwalimu played a critical role. As Chairman of the Frontline States, he assisted all the national liberation movements to wage armed liberation struggle, which culminated in the total liberation of our continent from the yoke of colonialism and foreign domination. This is one of his greatest achievements. His legacy of total commitment to social justice and progress in Africa, and the world at large, will endure for generations to come.

Thirdly, his commitment to unity within the country and African unity had an almost missionary zeal. To him the imperative of Unity, solidarity and cooperation between poor and weak countries in pursuit of greater democracy on a global scale, and the sovereign equality of nations was paramount. Mwalimu always told his political and economic interlocutors that we are no less human just because we are poor.

Further, we mourn and pray for Mwalimu because to us, Tanzanians, he was the beloved Father of the Nation, a title which only Mwalimu Nyerere, and nobody else before or after him, can or could have, for in this title is the embodiment of all that Mwalimu Nyerere meant to us Tanzanians. He founded Tanganyika and created Tanzania from a collection of more than 120 tribes under successive foreign rule into a proud and a united people with national cohesion and stability, which is unfortunately an exception rather than the norm in this troubled continent and region.

As we mourn his death, we honestly thank God for the life of Mwalimu, which he devoted to the service of our nation and our people.

Mwalimu was an outstanding intellectual. His thoughts and ideas on a just society based on human equality and dignity were the foundation of our national philosophy of socialism and self-reliance, and his writings and speeches on this philosophy are prominent in the studies of socio-economic development in Africa and elsewhere, be it in the spheres of development economics, rural development, education or other areas of social engineering, and this has unleashed a plethora of literature from social commentators and academicians all over the world.

He was such an honest intellectual and thinker that he was quick to admit when he made mistakes in his thinking, or in the implementation of his ideas. In a self-critique, referring to "The Arusa Declaration: Ten Years Later", he was the first to admit that Tanzania was no nearer the twin goals of being socialist or self-reliant. When criticized later in life for propounding a philosophy that has not been fully operationalized, his reply was, I quote: "The fact that there are fewer people who go to church than those who don't does not invalidate the truth in the message of Christianity, and that should not make the church feel irrelevant".

Indeed Tanzania today is far from what Mwalimu wanted it to be, but the national objectives of creating an egalitarian and self-reliant nation which Mwalimu left us, are as valid today, and perhaps even more relevant as they were thirty years ago.

For this fundamental legacy and other reasons we mourn him and continue to celebrate his life.

Mwalimu was extremely sensitive to the downtrodden, the weak, the disabled and powerless. He was very sensitive to plight of refugees and displaced persons. Under his leadership Tanzania was not only peaceful, thereby not generating refugees, but he made Tanzania home to everyone seeking political and personal refuge.

The legacy of Mwalimu will never die.

The President of the United Republic of Tanzania, H.E. Benjamin Mkapa assured that the legacy of Mwalimu would never die. We will do all in our power in order:

- to maintain national unity, concord and harmony;
- to prosecute the war on poverty, with even greater zeal and ensure the fruits of the war are shared as widely and equitably as possible among the downtrodden;
- to defend the union between Tanganyika and Zanzibar which he founded together with another beloved founding leader, the late Sheikh Abeid Aman Karume.

Dear friends, let me end my remarks by saying that we in Tanzania, and we in Africa have had the blessing of a great man, and a great leader as the founding father of our nation and our unity. He was a founding father comparable with all great names of World History. A man of integrity, of honesty, of principle and of personal modesty who recognised his duty for those poor and weak wherever they were in the world. The best way we can honour this great internationalist is to uphold and fight for all that he believed in. Tanzania will miss Mwalimu, and so will Africa and the world.

I thank you for your attention.

JULIUS NYERERE: STATESMAN, THINKER, HUMANIST

Nikolai Kosukhin

Julius Kambarage Nyerere is a leader of the type of Mahatma Gandhi, Sun Yatsen, Gamal Abdel Nasser, Kwame Nkrumah, and Leopold Sedar Senghor, who have earned their place in the history of mankind. Even his miscalculations, about which he repeatedly spoke himself, have special features; they were the mistakes of a pathfinder. He belonged to the leaders of a charismatic type, symbolizing the ideals and expectations of the people. We are not just discussing simply the statesman, but the leader-thinker, whose contribution to the development of the original *Ujamaa* concept, and the experience of independent development is a really great one. Therefore it takes some time to estimate in a fitting manner his role and weight in world history.

All post-colonial history of Africa and, above all, Tanzania, is associated with his name. The Nyerere epoch is the period of the struggle of African peoples for independence the construction of the national state, the search for ways of development, and the establishment of democratic foundations in Tanzania.

Nyerere's political biography is typical of many African leaders. He was born in 1922 in the northern part of the country at a small village not far from Musoma town, to the family of the chief of a small ethnic group, the Zanaki. After receiving secondary education, he entered Makerere University, Uganda, and in 1949-1952 studied history and sociology at Edinburgh University. During his studies, Nyerere was interested in politics, and got to know some future West African leaders of national liberation movements. Nyerere's *weltanschaung* was formed under the strong influence of Fabian Socialism. On his return home, he worked with the Tanganyika African Association, and for some time he worked as a teacher at a secondary school close to Dar es Salaam.

In 1954, he became the head of the Tanganyika African National Union (TANU). In 1960 he has was appointed the Chief Minister, and after the declaration of independence on December 9, 1961, the Prime Minister.

One year later he was elected the President of the country. Shortly afterwards, Julius Nyerere became known by the honourable title "Mwalimu" (teacher). In 1964 he became the President of the United Republic of Tanzania. In 1985, of his own free will, Nyerere stepped down as president. He believed that a leader should resign when he is still "intellectually and physically capable to transfer the power to his successor", which was, at the time, Ali Hassan Mwinyi.

Since the early days of independence, the TANU ruling party has called upon the people of the country to work persistently at raising the standard of living, and eliminating the poverty and backwardness inherited from colonialism.

Guided by Nyerere, TANU developed and adopted the plan of "nation-building", having in view the widespread use, under the socialist slogans, of such communal traditions as common work, mutual help and support still existing in African society.

As far back as in the period of national liberation struggle, Julius Nyerere advanced the idea of "African Socialism", which later evolved into a painful search for the ways of development for the newly emerged states. The Nyerere's theoretical concepts reflected the nation's urgent needs: the requirements of farmers, urban workers, the tiny national bourgeoisie and the intellectuals.

In May 1960, he published an article titled "The Future of African Nationalism", where he argues for the necessity of social revolution and creating of such a society, whose foundation would be the well being of all rather than the accumulation of the wealth by a few individuals. It means that the new national governments should be socialist in their views and actions.[1]

Nyerere expounded his ideas on the essence of Socialism at a conference on Pan-African Socialism, which took place in April 1962 in Dar es Salaam. His keynote speech was titled "Ujamaa: the Foundation of African

---

[1] Julius K. Nyerere, *Freedom and Unity. A Selection from Writings and Speeches 1952-65* (Oxford University Press, London, 1967), p. 174.

Socialism". The concept of *Ujamaa* (Familyhood) is among the most influential and interesting theories created by the ideologists of the national liberation movements. The main meaning of this word is the type of social organization, characteristic of the traditional African extended family. Nyerere opined that the traditional way of life in a community is the exact pattern for the social order, in other words, for socialism. Putting in the concept of *Ujamaa* the various contents depending on a concrete situation, he combined his economic and social-political views in a comprehensive ideology of development.

The reference to socialism as a means to development was intended to be a symbol of national cohesion and unity, an ideology of development, and a legitimisation of the new authority by ideological means. Many essential elements of the *Ujamaa* concept were exposed to change during the practical and theoretical activity of its author. The African socialism was intended to look for the synthetic theory within the channel of world social development and to encompassing all that mankind had created in the field of social sciences.

A special place in Nyerere's theoretical heritage occupies the work "The Arusha Declaration" and TANU's "Policy on Socialism and Self-Reliance". Many years after, Julius Nyerere still valued this work highly, saying that two books, the Bible and the Arusha Declaration, were always with him. He emphasised that the whole community should be self-sufficient both economically and socially, irrespective of the outer world. In his opinion, it would allow keeping the feeling of uniqueness in the environment of technical modernization, would speed up development, and would contribute to saving human and material resources.

In an effort to prevent the bureaucratisation and degeneration of the TANU and the Government top officials, a kind of a "Code of the Leadership" was embodied in the Arusha Declaration prescribing that no TANU or government leader should hold shares in any company; hold directorship in any privately owned enterprise; receive two or more salaries; own houses which he rents to others[1]. Later these clauses were extended to all TANU and Government officials and civil servants in the high and middle cadres.

It is opportune to mention here that one of the determining features of the *Ujamaa* concept is its "human", ethical nucleus. At the very onset of independence, Nyerere emphasised the need "to build an ethic of the nation"[1], which should be based on national spiritual traditions. This explains his definition of socialism as an attitude of mind.

In the *Ujamaa* theory the individual was put at the centre of development; therefore all plans of development should be measured by the criteria of their conformity to the real needs and requirements of the people. The disregard of the human factor, according to Nyerere's explanation, was the main cause of mistakes in the political line of Tanzanian leaders.

Given the existing in Tanzania of communal solidarity, and the practice of farmers' teamwork, a mass programme of action was launched aimed at building a new society under the banner of the *Ujamaa* theory. The creation of *Ujamaa* villages was conceived as a voluntary form of cooperation of the peasantry and pursued certain objectives.

It was presumed that the resettlement of the peasants on more fertile sites, integration of villages, and transition to new methods of management - all this in due course should increase labour productivity in agriculture and raise living standard.

The principles of self-management and initiative in *Ujamaa* should have transformed these villages into schools of political and cultural mass education, which would have made them a strong base of the state and society.

The creation of such villages envisaged the voluntary participation of the peasants in teamwork. However, during the campaign, this major principle was broken.

In 1973, the TANU National Executive Committee adopted the decision on resettlement of all peasants in *Ujamaa* villages as soon as by the end of 1976. In 1981, the number of registered villages has reached 8,180, and embraced 14 million people or 90 percent of all the rural population. But the main motive of the creation of these settlements, the ensuring of food self-sufficiency, has failed to materialize.

9

The Tanzanian experience of agrarian development has shown the complexity and ambiguity of application of communal traditional norms. The resistance of farmers to any form of state interference in the sphere of their production activity was the problem that Chama Cha Mapinduzi (CCM Revolutionary Party) confronted at the time of the creation of *Ujamaa* villages and at the introduction in them of the principles of collective production. The majority of the inhabitants of *Ujamaa* villages, not having any stimulus to expand agricultural production, continued to live in the old traditional way tilling mainly their individual plots of land. Many peasants refused to work on collective fields, abandoned villages, and some even abandoned agricultural activities. Moreover, it turned out that the level of production on individual farms was 75 percent higher than on collective plot.

Apparently, the failure of cooperation is not evidence of the non-feasibility of the *Ujamaa* programme. Probably, the main reason is that it was introduced prematurely on a national scale.

Nyerere himself critically estimated realisation of the results of the programme. In the work "The Arusha Declaration. Ten Years After", He wrote that the country was facing "many problems, which had to be solved, and mistakes, which should be corrected. But we are moving in the right direction".[2]

In many respects the country has achieved good results, in particular, in the development of social equality, education, health services, democratic participation in decision-making and public management, getting into the practice of socialist cooperation. The standard of living of the population, consumption of the basic food products and living necessities has risen.

However, within several years Tanzania will encounter economic difficulties. "Our efforts", wrote Nyerere, "should be commensurable to our difficulties. We cannot expect a speedy return for our work. We should be ready to find the remuneration for our efforts in extending national self-sufficiency and preservation of our independence in actions. There is a time of sowing and a

[2] See Nyerere J., *The Arusha Declaration. Ten Years after* (Dar es Salaam, 1977), p. 51.

time of harvesting. I am afraid, that for us the time of sowing is not over yet."[3]

Nyerere, characteristically, sensibly and objectively rated his contribution to the country's development. After the 24-year long presidency he stepped down as the Head of State retaining the post of the Chairman of the ruling Revolutionary party of Tanzania, and five years later left this position too. During the ensuing years, he lived in his native village of Butiama, worked on his own farm, and periodically took part in various political functions.

To make clearer what Tanzania has achieved under Nyerere's presidency, it is necessary to recollect what state the country was in at the moment of its independence in 1961. After 75 years of colonial domination, first by Germany and then by Great Britain, the national coffers were nearly empty. Old age came at 40 years. Quite curable deseases became the cause of mass mortality both amongst children and adults. The rate of infant mortality reached 250 per 1000. Only 26 percent of the land suitable for agriculture was cultivated, and the rest of it remained unused. Large areas became unsuitable for human settlement because of the proliferation of the tsetse fly. The whole population of the country was squeezed into only 10 percent of the territory. About 90 percent of the people were deprived of access to sources of clean water. Only about a half-dozen lucky individuals had received tertiary education. The basic primary schools course was only four years long, and attended by a very small percentage of the population.

These days, Tanzania is a country with one of the highest level of education in the Third World. Primary education (7 years) is officially compulsory and free of charge. The number of students in secondary and tertiary education establishments has increased considerably. Tanzania is highly rated among the developing countries for its successful programmes of adult education. The death rate has decreased sharply, and some diseases have been totally eradicated. Almost the whole has access to free medical care and access to sources of safe potable water. Life expectancy has increased from 40 to 52 years, and infant mortality has been greatly reduced.

---

[3] See Nyerere, *The Arusha Declaration*, p. 52.

Nyerere left to the successor a country uncommonly united and stable. The ethnic problems, which are common in many African countries as the main obstacle on the way to achievement of national unity, in Tanzania practically have been left behind.

Nyerere paid special attention to the development of a national language, Swahili. He has translated into this language some plays by William Shakespeare and has written his own poetry.

In addition, there were achievements beyond statistics, for example, the reputation of Tanzania in the world arena, its role and authority among the peoples struggling for economic independence and national unity welded out of the of the country's ethnic groups. And in all that the achievement, the merit of Julius Nyerere is to be found.

Nyerere, who was at the helm of the country since its independence, was a recognized standard bearer of the struggle for African liberation and a tireless champion of the idea of equitable economic relations between the rich North and the developing South. "Freedom and Unity" was the slogan of the Tanganyika African National Union founded by Nyerere, which led the country to independence. In December 1963, Tanganyika and the neighbouring island state of Zanzibar formed the United Republic of Tanzania, which has become one of the most successful examples of African federalism.

Independence gave Tanzania the opportunity to establish diplomatic relations with the other countries of the continent, and also with the USSR. The development of diplomatic and political links between Tanzania and the USSR was accompanied by expansion of economic, scientific and technical contacts.

In October 1969, Nyerere visited the Soviet Union. The joint Soviet-Tanzanian communiqué revealed the identity of views on such important international problems as the struggle for liquidation of colonialism and the termination of imperialist aggression. In March 1977, a visit by a Soviet state delegation to Tanzania took place. During the visit, agreements on trade, and cultural and scientific cooperation were signed.

Nyerere repeatedly emphasized that his country requires more from the world, than the world requires from her. In the first years of independence the foreign policy course of Tanzania was distinguished by support for the peoples of Southern Africa in their struggle for national liberation and elimination of the system of apartheid and racial oppression. The vigorous foreign political activity of Tanzania and its leader has won the country a well-deserved authority among the world community.

In 1987, Julius Nyerere was awarded the International Lenin Peace Prize.

Dar es Salaam hosted the headquarters of many national liberation movements. The fighters of the national liberation armies: FRELIMO (Mozambique), MPLA (Angola), ANC (South Africa), and the troops of the national liberation forces of Southern Rhodesia (Zimbabwe) were trained in camps located in Tanzania.

From 1977 to 1985, Nyerere was the Chairman of the Frontline States group. From 1988 to 1990 he was Chairman of the Commission on South-South Cooperation. Since March 1996, he had been the Chief International Mediator on the Settlement of the Ethnic conflict in Burundi. Practically, till the last days of his life, Nyerere indefatigably sought for peace in Africa and solution to its problems by exclusively political means.

At the end of 1997, in connection with Nyerere's 75th anniversary, Dar es Salaam University held the international theoretical conference on the theme: "Reflections on Leadership in Africa: Forty Years after Independence". Some reports were directly devoted to Nyerere and his contribution to the liberation of Africa and consolidation Tanzania into a nation. Two years later, on October 14, 1999, at 10.30 a.m. in St. Thomas Hospital, in London in the 78th year of his life, Julius Nyerere died.

Such was the outstanding figure of the national liberation movement of Tanzania, its first President Julius Nyerere. The man with a kind heart and a large destiny, he belongs not only to Tanzania and Africa, but also to all mankind. In the UN Secretary General's statement on the occasion of the death of the first President of Tanzania, he told the world that Julius Nyerere was a 20th century giant.

JULIUS NYERERE: THE THEORIST OF SOCIALIST ORIENTATION

Vassili Solodovnikov

My presentation is in two points. First, I wish to outline Nyerere's role as a theorist of the non-capitalist way of development in Tanzania. Secondly, I wish to tell you about my meeting with this outstanding figure of Africa.

Some of our "theorists" of the socialist orientation for African countries have failed to stand the test of time; they reneged on their former positions and, echoing western anti-Soviet propagandists, now charge the CPSU and Soviet scholars engaged in the problems of developing countries, with ostensibly imposing on the African people the theory of the socialist orientation, i.e. non-capitalist way of economic development for the least developed countries.

So what was the reality? Was the theory of socialist orientation imposed on African countries by the Soviet theorists, or was it a natural reflection of the real situation in the liberated African countries? Now, as in the past, I associate myself with those who believe that the socialist orientation in African post-independence countries was a law-governed response of the African leaders to the problems facing their people. The socialist orientation has been achieved by African people through suffering in the course of anti-colonialist struggle, the struggle against economic and political domination of the capitalist powers.

From the very onset, the anti-colonial struggle of the peoples of Africa assumed an anti-capitalist character, for in Africa, as well as in other parts of the world colonialism was associated in people's minds with capitalism and with the pro-racist policy of imperialism.

The leaders, and the educated class of the liberated countries, as a rule, were unwilling to accept capitalism as a model for their new social order. In 1966, Nyerere said that the United States instead of siding with the revolutionary parties, as it was required to be by history, always acted

14

in support of European colonialism. Up to now, the USA is moulding its African policy through London. [4] A similar view of American policy in Africa was also held by other leaders: Kwame Nkrumah, Modibo Keita, Sècou Turè, Gamal Ahmed Nasser, Agostinho Neto, Amilcar Cabral, and Samora Mashel.

The Soviet Union since the very first days of its existence, always, even during the most difficult years of the Second World War, was firmly and consistently on the side of anti-colonial movements. It supported these movements not only politically, but frequently rendered them material assistance. Thus, the USSR by the fact of its existence, example, and politics of support of the anti-colonial movements, influenced the formation of a pro-socialist ideology in the politically active part of the population of countries still under colonial rule, and those countries newly liberated from the colonial yoke.

Naturally, the USSR, including the professional Africanists and the author of this article, supported the pro-socialist option of the peoples of these countries. It would have been strange, if we, Marxists, had disputed this option and turned into advocates for a capitalist road. Facts testify that the leaders of African national liberation movements and the newly emerged countries, chose the socialist path of development on their own. One of such leaders was Julius Nyerere. He opted for socialism from the very outset. In 1961, Tanzania became independent. In 1962, Nyerere published a work: "Ujamaa: The Foundations of African Socialism", and in 1968 he published one more: "Freedom and Socialism", which comprised his articles and speeches over the period from 1965 to 1967. This book included such works, as "The Arusha Declaration", "The Varied Paths to Socialism", "Socialism and Rural Development".

I shall quote from an interview with Dr Nyerere in which he expresses some of his ideas about socialism, which was published in the "Times of Zambia" newspaper. Laurie Carrett, a correspondent, who had interviewed Julius Nyerere, wrote:

---

[4] See *Herald Tribune* (London), 24-25 February 1979.

"Tanzanian president Julius Nyerere is often regarded as one of the two or three most important leaders of the Third World, and certainly as a political giant of Africa. He is the acknowledged leader of the Frontline states and as such, has been the key personality in the African liberation movement for almost 20years. Dr. Nyerere is also the key theorist of 'African socialism"[5] Here are some excerpts from this interview:

Laurie Carrett, You have chosen to follow a socialist path of development for the Third World, not just in Africa. Tanzania socialism is obviously different from other forms. How would you describe its ideology?[6.]

Julius Nyerere,"I would describe our ideology as socialist.That's all.We're fighting against capitalism, all of us.We're trying to establish, I hope, just societies, healthy relationships between individuals.

We've started from different bases. I am not a Marxist. I do accept the economics of Marxism. I do not accept some of the philosophies of Marxism [Julius Nyerere, in particular, rejected the concept of class struggle. **V.S.**]

But even with the economics I have some difficulty. Classically, Marxism is socialism of the rich. It is a socialism, which starts with highly developed capitalism and highly developed proletariat.At present, it is the US, under Marxism, which (in Marxist eyes. V.S.) is really ripe for socialism. It has a proletariat, and this proletariat is the product of capitalism itself.

My problem is, having accepted socialism as the right development for my country, whether I should nurture capitalism until I have the proletariat. In Tanzania, the dominant class is not the proletariat; it's the peasants."[7] "Socialism here will have to be build using peasants.We have not inherited anything created by capitalism. We have to create wealth here. And so, starting [our movement to socialism, **V.S.**] from the different base [in comparison with Marxism, **V.S.**], our methodology is likely to be different. But I hope the objective is going to be the same."[8] "I hope",

---

[5] *Times of Zambia* (Lusaka), 24 November 1979.
[6] Ibid.
[7] Ibid
[8] Ibid

Nyerere continues, "we shall succeed with [our] methods of establishing human societies where human beings can live as human beings and not just be dominated by poverty. Property was never intended to dominate human beings. Wealth was never intended to live side by side with poverty, ever. Wealth was always intended to discover what light is to darkness; where there is wealth, poverty disappears; where there is light, darkness disappears. But capitalism succeeds to work out this miracle – that wealth can live side by side with poverty, because wealth is used as power."[9]

As one can see from this statement, non-Marxist Nyerere, a leader of the national liberation movement and the Head of an African state, speaks about the non-capitalist way to socialism in approximately the same words, which 46 years back, Marxist Vladimir Lenin used, substantiating the theory of a non-capitalist way of development.

On 26 July 1920, addressing a meeting of the Commission on the National Questions of the Second Congress of the Communist International, Lenin said:

"The question was posed as follows: are we to consider as correct the assertion that the capitalist stage of economic development is inevitable for backward nations now on the road to emancipation and among whom a certain advance towards progress is to be seen since the war? We replied in the negative."[10]

I do not know, whether Nyerere read Lenin's works and took proper account of the USSR's experience in socialist transformations, but his "African socialism" is a native brother of the Lenin's "non-capitalist way of development".

It is unlikely that on this basis anyone will venture to accuse Nyerere that

---

[9] *Times of Zambia* (Lusaka), 24 November 1979.
[10] V.I. Lenin, "The Second Congress of the Communist International", *Collected Works*, Vol. 31, p. 244

he has fashioned the ideology of the non-capitalist way of development under the pressure of the USSR or Soviet scholars. It was certainly his independent choice, the socialist choice of a non-Marxist, but a pragmatist who was taking into account the realities of the world development and those of his country, Tanzania.

Nyerere was not the only African leader, who perceived the concept of socialist orientation as the form of political structure for African countries. Such outstanding African leaders as Kwame Nkrumah, Modibo Keita. Sècou Turè, Kenneth Kaunda and others held the same point of view.

Kwame Nkrumah, in his book "Africa Must Unite", in the chapter "Construction of Socialism in Ghana", wrote: "in Ghana we have entered on a socialist way to progress ... Manufacture for the sake of private profit deprives a huge part of the population of the produced goods and services. Therefore, if we want to do our duty to the people and to carry out the planned programme, socialism for us is the only way." [11]. In another book – "Autobiography" – Nkrumah quotes the "Rules of the Convention Peoples Party (CPP)" (the revised edition of 1961), which reads that to create the prosperous state based on socialist system of a society with reference to Ghanaian conditions, the party realizes that African socialism, of the kind the Party has in view, cannot be achieved by one leap, for socialism is a form of the public structure based on a high level of industrialization and prospering agriculture. [12]

In Modibo Keita's collection of "Speeches and statements" one may read that the proponents of certain conceptions are frightened in hearing the word "socialism". But we are not afraid of it. Our socialism does not mean blind copying of experience of other countries. We shall always take into account the present-day reality. [13]

Though Sékou Touré did not speak directly bout socialism or about socialist orientation, but in the book, issued in 1966, "Africa and Revolution" (by the way, Sekou Toure has sent the book to this author

---

[11] See Kwame Nkrumah, *Africa Must Unite,* 1964/
[12] See Kwame Nkrumah, *Autobiography,* 1963
[13] See Modibo Keita, Selected Speeches M., 1964 (In Russian).

18

with his autograph) he wrote that in modern conditions, the developing countries should not necessarily pass classical phases of feudalism or capitalism, and based on this premise the leaders of the Democratic Party of Guinea (PDG) and Guinean government defined the ways of development of the country. In other words, Sékou Touré has asserted himself as an advocate of the theory of non-capitalist development.

There is every reason to assume that the leaders of these African countries have come to an understanding that the way out of the economic backwardness for their peoples is connected with the socialist option. I am not discussing now why their hopes have not materialised. It is a separate question and another theme. But what looks important to emphasize, is that these outstanding leaders have turned into the champions of African socialism, socialist orientation or non-capitalist way of development not because these theories were imposed on them by the Soviet ideology. It was their choice. But Soviet ideologists, politicians and scholars supported these ideas and provided their theoretical foundations. Being Marxists by convictions, they could not act otherwise. I, for one, trusted and continue to trust that socialism is the most equitable form of social organization.

We have cited here statements of the outstanding African leaders about a socialist choice for their countries relating to the 1960s. In our literature and in the CPSU official documents the theory of socialist orientation began to be seriously developed at the late 60s and early 70s. I think it is possible to say that our views on the socialist orientation were influenced not so much by Marxist dogma as by the statements of those and other leaders and theorists from the developing countries.

The Soviet scholars' concept of "socialist orientation" as an equivalent to the term of a non-capitalist way of development was used for the first time by a Yugoslavian researcher Dr Hajji Vasilieva in April 1966, at an International conference in Moscow on "The tendencies of economic and social development of the African countries". She put side-by-side the terms "non-capitalist way of development", "anti-capitalist way of development" and "socialist orientation".

The researchers of the Institute for African Studies and I personally, started to use in learned books and articles the term "socialist orientation" as an equivalent to the term "non-capitalist way of development". I wrote about it in the foreword to the book of a Beninese author Koawi Ouedago "Capitalism and Socialism in Africa", published by the "Progress" Publishing House in 1987.

There are all grounds to assert, that the western and domestic opponents of the theory of socialist orientation were too quick with its funeral. I am sure that the theory of socialist orientation, which the Soviet scholars, and, with reference to the conditions of Africa, Nyerere and other African leaders developed, will be acclaimed, for it provides the answer to the deep expectations and hopes of millions of people in the Third World in helping their countries out of economic backwardness and poverty.

And finally: the victory of the USA and its allies in the Cold War over the USSR is being paid with a too high price not only by the peoples of the USSR, but also by the overwhelming majority of the Third World countries. The gap in levels of economic well-being between the poorest part of the developing countries and the richest countries of the capitalist North has grown from 30 times in 1960 to 60 times now. Because of this the most urgent task of the world in the 21st century is the elimination of the chasm in living standards between the poor South and the super rich capitalist North. The solution of this global problem for the developing countries is possible only in the path to socialism.

My meeting with the President of Tanzania, Julius Nyerere, took place in the period from March 10 till March 16 1974, when I, as the head of the delegation of the Soviet Association of Friendship with the Peoples of Africa, was in Mauritius to celebrate the occasion of the anniversary of the independence of this country.

The delegation, apart from myself, was composed of Valentina Shevchenko, at that time the Chairman of the Ukrainian Association of Friendship, President of the Presidium of the Supreme Soviet of Ukraine and Vice-President of the Presidium of the USSR Supreme Soviet. Now Valentina Shevchenko is the head of the fund for Maternity and Child

Protection "Ukraine to Children" and is nicknamed by her protectees "the Ukrainian Mum". The third member of the delegation was Vladimir Tsvetkov, a one-time official of the International Department of the CPSU Central Committee. Subsequently he worked in the Solidarity Committee, and now he is in the Russian diplomatic service in Africa.

The delegation had many meetings with Mauritian statesmen and public figures, including one with the Prime Minister Sir Navin Ramgoolam.

On March 11, the second day after our arrival in the capital city of Port Luis, the delegation, among other foreign visitors, was invited to dinner to the Governor General, which he gave in honour of the President of Tanzania Julius Nyerere, who had also arrived to celebrate the Independence Day.

I found myself at the same table with the Chief of Protocol of the Ministry of Foreign Affairs of Tanzania, Mr À. B. Suedi, who acted as the chief of Protocol for the president of Tanzania. I told him that our delegation, after a short stay in Mauritius, would like to visit Tanzania. Considering what took place later, there was reason to assume, that Suedi shared this information with the Minister of Foreign Affairs, and, possibly, with the president of Tanzania.

On 13 March, the Governor General gave a reception in honour of Independence Day. At the reception, our delegation was accompanied by the counsellor of the USSR Embassy in Mauritius, Mr N. Dorodnitsin. He told me that the president of Tanzania, Julius Nyerere, is present at the reception. "Would you like to come and introduce yourself to him?" asked the counsellor. I immediately agreed with this offer. We found the ambassador of Tanzania to Mauritius, and the latter introduced me to President Nyerere as the head of the Soviet delegation, which was taking part in the celebration of Mauritius' Independence Day. I told the President about the Institute for African Studies of the USSR Academy of Sciences and about the Soviet Association of Friendship with the Peoples of Africa. Nyerere listened to me very attentively, sometimes asked questions. I, naturally, informed him about the Institute's research programmes, including both history and current events in Tanzania, and the experience of social transformations, which was initiated by its leader, Julius Nyerere. I cannot now recollect how long this conversation lasted. At the end of it Nyerere asked: "Why don't you visit Tanzania on your way home from Mauritius? We invite you to visit our country". I thanked the president for the invitation and told him that our delegation planned to arrive in Dar es Salaam on 18 March, and would, within 4-5 days try to get acquainted with the life of Tanzanian people. We also had in view the expansion and strengthening of contacts and cooperation with Tanzanian public organizations and the academic community.

As far as we could understand, the President was glad to hear this and said several times: "It's good, it's very good".

I thought that on that note, our conversation was over. I once again thanked the president for the invitation to visit Tanzania, adding that I was glad to get acquainted to its President, and already at that point was about to take my leave. But the President grasped my hand, looking for someone among the crowd of visitors. Soon we approached the Minister of Foreign Affairs, Mr J.S Malechela, who was asked by the President to send to Dar es Salaam the necessary instructions and to accord a warm welcome to our delegation. I specified the purpose of our visit, and told the minister that we would like to negotiate the expansion of cooperation between public organizations of our countries. I also told him that we would like to visit one of the *Ujamaa* villages to learn at first hand the experience of social transformation in Tanzanian society, about which we knew only from reading books and articles. We also told him that we would like to get acquainted with the structure and research programmes of the Dar es Salaam University. After an exchange of farewell greetings, I said Good Bye to Nyerere.

That is how I first got acquainted with the President of Tanzania. This brief meeting with him elevated the status of our delegation in Tanzania. We were announced as guests of the government.

In Tanzania any door was opened to us, for we were considered as the personal guests of the President.

At the Dar es Salaam airport our delegation was met by the USSR Ambassador to Tanzania Sergei Slipchenko, the representatives of the Ministry of International Affairs, and the Ministry for Information and Broadcasting. While still at the airport we were told that our delegation had been declared official guests of the Minister for Information and Broadcasting Mr Daudi Mwakawago, who was also TANU's publicity secretary. Later Slipchenko told me that he was amazed to learn that the Tanzanians had shown such an intense interest in the Soviet delegation. The Ministry for Information and Broadcasting suggested that in cooperation with the Soviet embassy, they would draw up a joint programme to be followed by the delegation during their stay in Tanzania. A meeting with the ministers and an official dinner hosted by the Minister for Information and Broadcasting was included in the programme. Only after I had told Slipchenko of my meeting with President Nyerere in Port Luis, did he understand the reason of the warm reception accorded to the Soviet delegation. On the morning of March 19, the Minister for Information and Broadcasting received our delegation. We informed him about the purpose of our visit to Tanzania, and finally coordinated the programme of our stay. Ambassador Slipchenko accompanied us to all functions.

We visited the Minister for Planning and Economic Development, Dr Chagula, who simultaneously chaired the National Committee on Scientific Researches, and was the President of the East African Academy of Sciences. The delegation also visited and held conversations with the Minister of Education Mr Chiwanga, at TANU headquarters; it was the TANU Assistant Organisation Secretary, Mr F.M. Rungina, who received us. In the headquarters of the OAU Liberation Committee we met and negotiated with the Executive Secretary of this Committee Hashim Mbita, and the OAU Assistant Executive Secretary for defence, Mr A. Sidiki (Egypt).

The subject of the negotiations was the problems of the national liberation movement in Africa, specifically in Portuguese colonies and Southern Rhodesia. At all meetings there was an intensive exchange of opinions on bilateral cooperation between our countries and on other problems of Africa.

The round table discussions with lecturers of Dar es Salaam University were especially interesting and useful to our delegation. The problems of the liquidation of economic backwardness in the countries of Africa, questions of the theory and practice of transformation of Tanzanian society on the *Ujamaa* foundation (an official ideological concept of the *Chama Cha Mapinduzi*, The Revolutionary Party, which rejects capitalism, private property and exploitation of man by man) were at the centre of our discussions.

On 20 March, the Minister of information gave a dinner in honour of our delegation. Present were the Ministers of Information and Broadcasting, the Minister of Planning and Economic Development, the Minister of Youth and Sports, the Minister of Education, the Vice-Chancellor of the university and other high-ranking officials.

On 21 March, we visited an agricultural area, where we met local leaders, and party operatives, and talked to cooperative farmers in *Ujamaa* villages. We had no difficulties in these open and franc discussions, as our interlocutors knew that we had been invited to Tanzania by President Nyerere himself.

Our delegation's stay in Tanzania was widely covered by the local press.

The memories of my meeting with Nyerere, and the warm reception accorded to our delegation in Tanzania have remained with me all my life. First of all, I remember so vividly Julius Nyerere, wise statesman and politician, courageous theorist, one of the authors of the concept of "African socialism". Despite of high position in the state, I remember him as a modest and accessible man, ready for meetings and conversations with any interlocutor, who showed an interest in Africa, the destiny of the peoples of this continent, and their future.

I believe, Nyerere also found the meeting with the Soviet scholar and public figure interesting, especially, when I told him that we wanted to get acquainted at ground level with the socio economic transformations taking place in Tanzanian villages on the *Ujamaa* basis. Probably, it was his first informal meeting with a Soviet professional Africanist.

I was deeply impressed with his simplicity and democratic attitude. To make sure that that I did not get lost among the crowd, he took me by the hand, and together we began to search for the Minister of Foreign Affairs. He was surrounded by assistants and bodyguards, and it was only necessary for him to say the word, and they would have done this for him, but he didn't do that. He went to search for the minister himself. This simple, generous behaviour showed me that Julius Nyerere, a man with great authority, remained a democrat, a Man with a capital M, and such I have always remembered him.

Nyerere was, and remains in history as one of the outstanding figures of the national liberation revolution in Africa, outstanding leader of the state, who ventured to reject capitalism and private property and to make a socialist choice.

And finally, to finish my story, I shall mention one more fact.

In early 1976, through the Soviet embassy in Tanzania, I sent to President Nyerere an Art album "Art of the peoples of Africa", prepared by the researchers of the Institute for African Studies. On 8 April 1976, Nyerere's private secretary, J. Butiku, sent a letter to the USSR Ambassador to Tanzania, Mr. Sergei Slipchenko, which read: "Allow me, on behalf of President Mwalimu Julius K. Nyerere to express his gratitude for your letter of March 12, 1976, with which you forwarded the book "Art of the peoples of Africa", and for the letter from the Chairman of the Soviet Association of Friendship with the Peoples of Africa. On behalf of the President, I would like to ask you to express to the Chairman of the Soviet Association of Friendship with the Peoples of Africa his gratitude for the letter and the gift of the book and, above all, for that interest, which is shown by the Soviet people in various aspects of life of our people".

Our conference, devoted to the life and activity of the outstanding son of Africa, Julius Nyerere, is being held on the 40th anniversary of the "Africa's Year", the 40th anniversary of the adoption of the declaration on granting independence to the countries and peoples, the 40th anniversary of the founding of the Institute for African Studies, the 41st anniversary of the establishment of the Soviet Association for Friendship with the

Peoples of Africa. All these events, which took place in the year 1960, are interconnected, and all of them have resulted from the anti-colonial revolutions in Africa.

Summing up my recollections, I would like to add that the academic staff of the Institute for African Studies of the USSR Academy of Sciences, and the active workers of the Soviet Association for Friendship with the Peoples of Africa have made an essential contribution to the strengthening of the friendship and mutual understanding between the peoples of the USSR and the countries of Africa. The activity of these organizations promoted the strengthening of the influence of the USSR and its foreign policy on the African continent.

One of the most belligerent among the USA anti-Soviet propagandists, David E Albright, senior text editor of the Washington-based quarterly "Problems of Communism" and the author of a book "Africa and the International Communism" was compelled to recognize this. In an article "Soviet Policy in Southern Africa" he wrote,

'Moscow's assets now include a pool of academic specialists on Africa who not only turn out substantial quantities of writings about Africa but also engage in dialogue with the political and intellectual elite of the continent through correspondence, exchange visits, conferences, and other activities.[14]

The visit of the delegation of the Soviet Association of Friendship with the Peoples of Africa to Mauritius and Tanzania confirmed in full measure this conclusion of the American Sovietologist.

---

[14] *African Index* (Washington), Nov. 3. 1980. Vol. III. No 19, p. 72/

NYERERE'S TIME
(In memory of the first President
of the United Republic of Tanzania)

Vyacheslav Ustinov

This outline does not claim to be a study of concrete aspects of the history of Tanzania. I only wish to give a parting tribute to eminent politician, and outstanding citizen of Tanzania, Julius Kambarage Nyerere, who passed away on the 14 October, 2000. He made his mark on the history of the entire African continent. I want to share my impression of this great man and political figure. I had the chance to meet him on many occasions through almost two decades. In our contacts and talks we broached a wide array of problems beyond the range of pure politics, for example, questions of literature, in which Julius Nyerere showed a keen interest. Suffice it to say that he was the first Tanzanian to translate into Swahili some works of Shakespeare. I wish to confide to you my recollections and thoughts about this unordinary man, which have been preserved by my imperfect human memory.

How did all this begin? About 40 years ago, in January 1962, a month and a half after Tanganyika had obtained its independence, a small group of the Soviet diplomats, including the present author, set out on their journey to Dar es Salaam via London.

To sort out some problems with British and Tanganyika representatives, we had to stay in London for a short while. We informed them that the Soviet diplomatic mission in Dar es Salaam would be headed by a chargé d'affaires, until the proper conditions were created for the normal functioning of the embassy.

One week later, we departed for Tanganyika's capital, and here we were flying above the African continent. We saw the wide expanses of desert and savannah, on which, hardly perceptible from such a great height, moved huge herds of wild animals. Our intermediate flight stop was in Nairobi, the capital city of Kenya, still at the time British colony. - Our pilot deliberately flew over the majestic Mount Kilimanjaro, so that we could see the crater of an extinct volcano. There, actually, something was sparking brightly, as if it was a mirror-like surface under the sun.

Then, we crossed the equator, and on this occasion the aircraft commander presented each of us with the appropriate certificate. Finally, our plane landed in the territory of Tanganyika, in the town of Arusha, located rather high above sea level. The mild climate there is very pleasant. The wooded slopes of Kilimanjaro, and sheer quantity of the flowers and trees make the Arusha landscape very picturesque.

By the way, Kilimanjaro is the highest mountain in Africa, and moreover, it is the only one covered with glaciers. Tanganyika can also boast of the largest African lakes, and the Serengeti National Park. When a drought comes, millions of wild animals migrate from Kilimanjaro to the Great lakes, and during the rainy season, in the opposite direction. Those who have seen this great migration if only once in their lives, will never forget it.

At last, we arrived in Dar es Salaam, and were put up at the Hotel Twiga (giraffe in Swahili).

Despite the multitude of ethnic groups in Tanganyika (about 120), most people understand Swahili, and this language has, probably, helped its inhabitants to preserve relatively calm interethnic relations in contrast to their neighbours. The Swahili language has absorbed synthetically the local Bantu vernaculars and borrowings from Arabic. In the Middle Ages, Arab and Persian traders colonized the Indian Ocean coast of East Africa and Swahili became the main means of communication. Now tens of millions people use this language in Tanzania, Kenya and the Democratic Republic of Congo.

Without delay we plunged in our working routine: renting a car, depositing money in a bank, which, strange as it may sound, we had brought with us in a travelling bag. We then paid a visit on the Governor General of the country, which, despite of independence, remained part of the British Commonwealth.

The Prime Minister was Rashidi Kawawa, and I handed over to him the note of my accreditation as the chargé d'affaires before arrival of the ambassador. We started to look for suitable buildings, both for the embassy office, and residential apartments for the embassy staff.

At that time, the quota of diplomats for all diplomatic missions, except the member states of the British Commonwealth, was limited to ten persons. But Dar es Salaam was not then a big town, and the embassies were mushrooming. Therefore to find suitable buildings was not an easy task. We employed a driver, Waziri Suleimani, who, despite his youth, appeared skilled, and knew the city like the back of his hand. He quickly got us acquainted with Dar es Salaam and its environs. [As an aside, Waziri remained as our unchangeable driver ever since that first appointment, and served faithfully three subsequent ambassadors most faithfully. He died by no means old man. Blessed be his memory!].

And now, I would like to mention, in retrospect, the events previous to my first arrival in Tanganyika.

The leader of the Tanganyika African National Union (TANU), Julius Kambarage Nyerere, the head of the country's national liberation movement, was born in 1922 (according to other information, in 1921) in northern Tanganyika, to the family of Chief Burito, who headed a small tribe the Zanaki. Nyerere studied at local schools, then at Makerere University, Uganda. He became the first Tanganyikan, to be admitted to Edinburgh University and graduated there with a Master of Arts degree. In his student years, he took a keen interest in the problem of colonialism. And though, when he came home, he started working as a teacher, it soon became clear that he was preparing himself for a political career.

In 1953, Nyerere became the President of the Tanganyika African Association, and on July 7, 1954, he founded and became the head o the Tanganyika African National Union (TANU). It is possible to consider this date as the beginning of the struggle by peaceful means for Tanganyika's independence. Setting aside all peripetias and peculiarities of the anti-colonial struggle, it is worth mentioning that before long Nyerere became the most authoritative political figure in the country.

In October 1960, Nyerere became Chief Minister in the colonial administration, and then, Prime Minister, when internal self-government was granted in May 1961.

On 9 December 1961, Tanganyika was proclaimed independent, though the country for one year retained a British Governor General, and technically, the Head of State was the Queen of England.

On 22 January 1962, Nyerere resigned as prime minister to concentrate, as we would say, on party building, in connection with preparation for the presidential elections, which were held in December 1962. The same month Tanganyika became a republic, with Nyerere as its first President. Nyerere's lifelong colleague, Rashidi Kawawa, became the Prime Minister of the country.

In those years, Dar es Salaam was a small city picturesquely stretched along the coast of the Indian Ocean. It had, at that time, a Hindu-Pakistani flavour, since the Hindus and Pakistanis made up over a half of population there. These ethnic groups handled the bulk of trade and owned a number of plantations. The Europeans were not numerous, mainly officials of the colonial administration, and a few planters. The Africans huddled together on the outskirts in their traditional huts.

As we were staying in a hotel in the city centre, we quickly got acquainted with the local elite, and in a few days I had met Nyerere for the first time. It happened in our hotel's restaurant. I noticed an African, sitting at the nearest table. It is worth mentioning, that in the first post-independence months Africans were not frequent diners in restaurants. Our neighbour was a lean person, of medium height, with live clever eyes, sporting a short Chaplinesque moustache. He was dressed in a dark blue "safari suit", which later on, after some updating, became his everyday wear. I noticed that he also was watching my companions and me with marked interest. He was sitting at a table with an official from the British administration, with whom I was already acquainted. The latter presented me to Julius Nyerere, Mwalimu (the "teacher" as he is known in Swahili). He was a smiling good-natured man interested in everything and everybody, and had a very attractive sense of humour. He showed a genuine interest in

1969 Moscow, Visit of the President of Tanzania J. Nyerere to the USSR. J. Nyerere placed the wreath of flowers at the Mausoleum of Vladimir Lenin.
Photo by V. Runov.

1969 Leningrad, Visit of the President of Tanzania J. Nyerere in the USSR. J. Nyerere signs the book of guests of honour in Piskarev Memorial Cemetry in Leningrad. *Photo by V. Runov.*

1969 Moscow, Visit of the President of Tanzania J. Nyerere to the USSR. Reception for the honour of Julius Nyerere and the heads of diplomatic representations acredited in Moscow. President of Tanzania greats the Director of the Institute of African Studies (USSR) V. G. Solodovnikov.

1969 Leningrad, Visit of the President of Tanzania J. Nyerere t the USSR. Nyerere in the memorium room of Vladimir Lenin in Smolny Palace in Leningrad.
Photo by V. Runov.

life in our country, asked about Moscow, and even said, that at a later date (when Tanganyika was fully independent), he would like to pay a visit to the USSR.

As far as I remember, during the first conversation not a word was uttered about socialism, communism, or capitalism. But what really amazed me was his critical rating of his fellow citizens. I am sure, he said, that the Americans will go into space, and, possibly, to the moon, the Russians will go into space and to the moon, but the Tanzanians in the foreseeable future will not go anywhere. We must run, while other peoples can quietly walk. But our citizens do not want it, for they are lazy. But it is not their laziness, as the objective conditions do not allow them to reach such heights. We continued this conversation at the evening reception, where we met again. Later I came to learn that such pronouncements were a leitmotif of Nyerere's talks with many people from different countries.

A couple years later, a book on Nyerere was published in America under the title: "We must run, while they walk"[15].

I told Nyerere that even that little, which I had a chance to see in Tanganyika, had shown me that the country has fertile land, and a great opportunity for the development of tourism that could promote the Africans' living standards.

What arrested my attention in Nyerere, even after a superficial acquaintance with him, was his erudition and that special sort of upbringing, which allowed him to comport himself with a natural, instead of an affected simplicity. Add to this the natural sense of humour, and it becomes clear what a pleasant impression this man made on me.

In such a way, our first acquaintance took place, and our friendship lasted, off and on, up to the early 1980s. I do not want the reader to get an impression that everything went swimmingly. There were difficulties, disappointments, not everything turned out as was expected or desired. It should be remembered that ambassadors come and go, and that

---

[15] See Smith, William Edgett. *We must run while they walk*. N.Y. 1971.

views of Nyerere's team also changed. Sometime later, a shift appeared towards the ideas of Mao Zedong, though it did not bode well for Tanzania. The Soviet leaders, in their turn, treated Nyerere with some mistrust. Nevertheless, I do not remember a single occasion where we did not find mutual understanding at a personal level.

The year 1962 was devoted to the preparation for the declaration of Tanganyika as a republic and for presidential elections, which brought Nyerere to his office in December 1962. A great many people saw off the last Governor General and other British officials at the harbour. A thunderous salvo announced the birth of the independent Republic of Tanganyika. The Africans triumphed, the Whites, mostly British nationals, accepted it with a stiff upper lip. The numerous, especially in the capital, Hindus and Pakistanis were ill at ease. They possessed a significant part of the sisal and other crops plantations. It should be remembered that, at the time, Tanganyika was the world's first producer of sisal, the most important fibre used for making ropes.

One day, Nyerere invited several heads of diplomatic missions, including myself, to visit some areas of the country. It was an interesting trip, not so much for what we were able to see, as in the ideas of the pending fundamental transformations in the country that Nyerere and two of his companions confided to us. First of all, as he said, it is necessary to find the teachers, for the overwhelming number of the population is illiterate, and to establish the foundation of health care services. If my memory does not fail me (unfortunately, I did not keep a diary), he developed his ideas of African socialism and, obviously, expected to get assistance from the USSR, the People's Republic of China and the Scandinavian countries.

During the trip on open cross-country vehicles, we stopped to spend the night in African huts, ate African food and almost forgot the amenities of civilization.

For the first time, I became a witness of Nyerere's meetings with the people, and though I did not understand Swahili (an interpreter helped me out), it was not important. Nyerere proved to be a brilliant public speaker who knew his people. The speech frequently switched off to an open dialogue with the audience. Indeed, it seemed that the teacher (Mwalimu)) was talking to his pupils.

After one of these meetings, we were having our supper at the veranda of a house. Nyerere confided to us his cherished dream: if Tanganyika by the turn of the century had achieved the then standard of living of one of the poorest of the European countries, he would be happy. I remember he has named Portugal and Greece as examples of such countries, and then he added ruefully: "But I am afraid, most likely, it will not happen". And, alas, he was right.

Later, during his visit to Tanzania, the Prime Minister of Sweden Olaf Palme (the Scandinavian countries during this period had begun a mass investment campaign in the economy of Tanzania), made the remark that East Africa (Kenya Tanzania, Uganda) in the next century could become the Europe's main granary. Nyerere replied jokingly:"I am afraid it may be quite the opposite".

The trip enabled us to get closer acquainted with Nyerere, and his associates, Tanzanians and their country. With some of Nyerere's team-mates I was able to establish friendly relations. From this trip I drew some conclusions. We often develop an involuntary inner bias towards Africans, without taking into account their way of life and the peculiarities of their countries' development. To be able to grasp their train of thought and sentiments it is necessary, so to say, to plunge into their midst and to take into account their values and perceptions.

It is worth mentioning also that many simple and even illiterate Africans are endowed with a keen mind and original wisdom; besides, they are extremely sensitive.

Many leaders of the national liberation movements of the countries, which had not yet gained their independence, had set up their headquarters in Dar es Salaam with the active support of the Tanzanian authorities.

This was a very interesting time for the diplomats working then in Tanzania. They had the opportunity to get acquainted with the future leaders of the neighbouring countries still under colonial yoke. Dar es Salaam frequently hosted the future president of Zambia Kenneth Kaunda, the president of Angola Agostinho Neto, future presidents of Mozambique Samora Mashel and Joaquim Chissano, who is still the head of state. The assistance on the part of Nyerere and his team has undoubtedly accelerated the liberation process, especially in the east and south of Africa.

Nyerere stood up for creation of the East African Federation consisting of Kenya, Tanganyika, Uganda, and Zanzibar. But this project was fated never to be realized, although Tanganyika and Zanzibar have united nevertheless. On the 22 April 1964, the President of the Republic of Tanganyika, Julius Nyerere, and President of the Peoples Republic of Zanzibar and Pemba, Abeid Karume, signed up an agreement to unite the two countries.

In the dead of night, the Minister of Foreign Affairs and Defence of Tanganyika, Mr Oscar Kambona, called me on the phone and asked me to come to his house urgently (we lived just across the road). Kambona informed me about just completed union and asked, what would be the reaction of the Soviet government.

I answered that now it is difficult for me to give an immediate explicit answer on behalf of my government. However, as the peoples of the two countries aspired to association, and it, undoubtedly, would strengthen the positions of progressive anti-colonial forces, it would undoubtedly be welcomed.

In such a key I have sent the message in Moscow and soon received the instruction to congratulate the leaders of the new allied state. On 25 April, this agreement was ratified, and the new state was first referred to as the United Republic of Tanganyika and Zanzibar. Later, the country was called the United Republic of Tanzania with Julius Nyerere as its President and Abeid Karume as the First Vice-President. The Second Vice-President was Rashidi Kawawa.

Since that time, Nyerere has become increasingly engaged in external political activities. In 1963, he vigorously supported the creation of the Organization of African Unity. The domestic policy of TANU focused on socialism and self-reliance. In 1967, the Arusha Declaration was adopted, which has constitutionalised these norms. Special emphasis was laid on the development of socialist *Ujamaa* villages, to which the peasants, unfortunately, were frequently driven by force. At this stage, it became clear that an attempt to construct a "Welfare Society" had suffered a crash.

In May 1966, I left for Moscow, and for three years my dialogue with this country was limited, basically, to meetings with the Tanzanian Ambassador, Mr Mfinanga, a faithful supporter of the president. Apparently, the situation in the country was far from ideal.

In September 1969, I was appointed the USSR ambassador to the United Republic of Tanzania with instruction to urgently prepare the visit of President Nyerere in the Soviet Union. The time of the visit was quickly coordinated, and I had to depart in Tanzania without delay. Nyerere was looking forward to such state visit, so it was easy and pleasant to work with him.

And here I am in Dar es Salaam again, as though I had never left it, but already in new ambassadorial premises, which my predecessor had constructed, but had no time to render habitable.

On the second day, contrary to the usual practice of waiting for two to three weeks, I, in my new white full-dress uniform, handed over to the president my credentials. We emptied the traditional glass of champagne, and at once plunged into a discussion about the forthcoming visit.

In a few days' time, I set off for Moscow to be, as the protocol prescribes, among the officials involved in hosting the president. State visits are always intense: negotiations and meetings, finding out the probable spheres of expansion of cooperation. A lot of time was spent on coordinating the comprehensive joint communiqué, a document that outlined those issues, on which our countries had common positions.

A large amount of time was needed also to persuade our Tanzanian counterparts to support us on a line of other questions. Only during the sightseeing tour to Leningrad was it possible to talk on more abstract themes.

Nyerere was pleased with the results of the visit. I told him that I was also pleased to start my ambassadorship with such an important event. During the visit Nyerere did not meet with Leonid Brezhnev. The president did not complain, but his minister of foreign affairs had hinted, that such meeting would be advisable. Why this meeting never occurred? I do not know, but the rumour was that Mikhail Suslov and some other Politburo members were against it. I, for one, made a note that in the future on the future, I would, if possible, address myself directly to the King, rather than to his counsellors.

Later, after my return from Tanzania, another similar case nearly occurred (though, the objective reasons here were weightier) with the president of Zambia, Kenneth Kaunda, who, arriving on an official visit to the USSR in 1974, learned that the next day Brezhnev was leaving Moscow for the Far East for a meeting with the American President Gerald Ford.

On realizing that his meeting with the CPSU General Secretary would not take place, Kaunda declared that he would not even leave the plane, but would go straight back home. Against the advice of certain officials, I telephoned one of Brezhnev's assistants. It was Aleksandrov-Agentov, as I recall. He put me straight through to Brezhnev, on a special line. Brezhnev started inquiring questions about President Kaunda, and I believed he would really carry out his threat to terminate the visit before it had even begun. I replied that according to my fairly longstanding knowledge of him, he is a quite intelligent man, but very touchy and impulsive, and such a turn of events must not be ruled out.

Grumbling that he would not have enough sleep before the important meeting with President Ford, Brezhnev, unwillingly agreed to brief conversation with President Kaunda with very few aid present. The meeting was held. It turned into a very interesting discussion, and lasted much longer than was intended. Brezhnev has admitted that he has been right to follow my advice, and Kaunda was in seventh heaven, and always welcomed me warmly whenever I visited Lusaka.

After this meeting with the General Secretary, a perfectly happy Kaunda, arriving in Tbilisi, part of the visit's official itinerary, arranged an amateur concert and took part in the even himself by playing the guitar.

But let us return to my three-year ambassadorship in Tanzania. Despite a host of complexities, our relationship with Nyerere remained good. As a result of his visit to the USSR, many Soviet experts in different fields: geologists, teachers, military experts, and others were sent to Tanzania. If the Soviet government agencies had been more efficient, and less West-oriented, our links with Tanzania could have brought more positive results for both countries. The work was so interesting that three years flashed like one day. Despite the growing difficulties, Nyerere and his team undertook desperate efforts to lead the country by their "African way". They wanted to create a civilised environment in the country. They wanted to dismantle the colonial mentality and to overcome the centuries, nay, thousands of years of backwardness. Their, to me, peculiar psychology was to live on a minimum. It was an arduous and complex process. While education and health care improved somewhat, the economy was in tatters. All this was a subject for hot discussions while possible solutions were searched for.

At the same time, Tanzania was increasingly becoming the centre of the national liberation movements. The neighbouring countries, one by one, became independent. These processes were already irreversible. We were witnessing how, despite all the odds against them, not only Tanzania but also the whole southern part of the African continent was undergoing a radical transformation.

Apart from political matters, we very much enjoyed our journeys through Tanzania and the neighbouring countries. The serenity of the scenery along the Indian Ocean coast near Dar es Salaam, never failed to delight us. We found enchantment in our conversations with people from so many ethnic groups, from the giant Masai to Pygmies, all of four foot tall. We were glad not to be made to feel like aliens in the country.

37

Immediately after our first arrival in the country, we accepted, as a member of our family, a young girl, Adida, our daughter's nursemaid. She spoke only one language, Kiswahili.

In the course of my duty, I have done a lot of travelling, in almost all continents of the world, but I have always kept a special warm spot in my heart for Africa and, especially, Tanzania.

In December 1972, I came back to the Ministry of Foreign Affaires, and was assigned to head the Department of East and Southern Africa countries. In this position I have visited Tanzania several times. What struck my eye was the ever-growing poverty and the disappearance of the enthusiasm, which was so prominent in the heyday of independence.

Julius Nyerere in his book "Ten years After the Arusha Declaration", published in 1977, wrote, with a touch of bitterness, that he had proved to be a poor prophet, for in the ten years after the Arusha declaration Tanzania had failed to attain economic independence. The material inequality between the rich and the poor is still great. But he also talks about some of the successes achieved during these ten years, and expresses hope that, when Tanzania commemorates the twentieth anniversary of the Arusha declaration, the production will have gathered momentum, and the country will have obtained more economic freedom.

In the spring of 1977, the Chairman of the Presidium of the USSR Supreme Soviet, or the President by African standards, Nikolai Podgorny, paid his first and, unfortunately, last visit to the countries of Africa, Tanzania included.

Negotiations between Julius Nyerere and Nikolai Podgorny took place as usual in the accepted framework. According to the programme, there were to be official negotiations as a body, negotiation in groups, a trip to a national park, and a meeting with the Soviet nationals in the country. Incidentally, Podgorny was not feeling well, and did not take part in the visit to the National Park.

The members of Nyerere's team told me that their president had appraised Podgorny's visit as an important one. There was an expectation that the visit would promote the expansion of Soviet assistance to Tanzania, but for Nyerere, even more essential was the idea that the visit was considered as recognition of Tanzania's socialist orientation. Nyerere said he would like to go to the USSR once again, having in view, among other things, a meeting with Leonid Brezhnev, which was not possible during the first visit in 1969.

However, none of this was to be. Nyerere never had a chance to visit Moscow again. Friction in the Soviet leadership led to sending Podgorny to retirement, almost immediately after the African trip. And though the trip, which was necessary, and on a number of ways even successful, had no relation to the Podgorny's resignation, both in the USSR and in the African countries the resignation left an unpleasant aftertaste. There was even an impression that the Soviet leadership was dissatisfied with Podgorny's visit to Africa. At that time no one took the pains to analyze, or separate these events.

Podgorny's visit gave me my last opportunity to closely communicate with Nyerere and his team. Later, we were to meet by chance in New York to take part in a UN peacekeeping function.

In 1985, Nyerere, having devoted his life to over 35 years of service to his country, voluntarily stepped down from the post of the president of Tanzania. This kind of decision is an exception on the African continent. However, for the next five years he remained the chairman of the ruling Chama Cha Mapinduzi, Revolutionary party, and continued to exert a significant influence on the country's development.

Despite of unsuccessful, often utopian, attempts to improve life in the country, which failed not only because of objective circumstances, but also because of pressures from the outside, Tanzanians have retained a profound respect for Nyerere, their "Mwalimu", to the last days of his life, and consider him the Father of the Nation.

Unlike many other African leaders, Nyerere was known for the integrity and modesty in his personal life. Even when he was the president, he preferred to work and rest in a small house on the shores of the ocean, where I, as well as some other diplomats, had a chance to visit him. The house was like a medium-size country-house, or "dacha" in Russian, a far cry from the size and splendour of the palaces belonging to modern 'New Russians'.

I remember especially one day at his house. When I, by prior arrangement, arrived at the house, Nyerere was not feeling well. Nevertheless, our expected conversation took place, but not in his study-room. Instead, I was ushered into the dining room, where there was a couch, on which he was reclining. The doctor arrived. I went out onto veranda and, but for the majestic ocean, I really could have imagined myself in a dacha in the Moscow suburbs. Nyerere used to say that his official residence, the former Governor General's Palace, was somewhat oppressive and made him feel ill at ease.

The Western mass media also rated Julius Nyerere as one of the African statesman with high moral principles repeatedly shown by his decisions on many important issues.

To be sure, Nyerere's stepping down from an active political life symbolized the failure of his polices, and caused a feeling of resentment towards his fellow Tanzanians. I can recollect one incident. Once, in the 1960s, in the presence of foreigners, Nyerere bitterly and even with anger remarked that it is impossible to speak about rapid development of the country, when the majority of the population is keen not on work, but on dancing. The owners of plantations of sisal, coffee and other crops paid the workers a mere pittance, which, it is necessary to remember, the majority of Africans have never even seen. It seemed that the workers on the plantations should go on strike, but it never happened. The workers were satisfied with the little money necessary to support their families, and then they returned in their villages, and the planters had to employ new workers. The only tangible progress achieved in the East African countries is the population explosion. By the year 2000 the population increased threefold, despite deceases, poverty and all the other hardships.

Perhaps, the most impressive Nyerere's successes were achieved in the social sphere. The rate of adult literacy rose from 20 percent at independence to 85 percent by 1990. In addition, the most impressive hospitals and health centres were built during Nyerere's presidency.

But the main achievement of Nyerere was the successful creation on the African continent of a federal state, which has outlived its founders. Besides, in contrast to many of his neighbours, he has ensured decades of a quiet peaceful life for his people.

Ten years of life without Nyerere as President have not made Tanzanians wealthier or freer. The International Monetary Fund and other financial institutions, to which the new Tanzanian leaders have applied for assistance, have failed to improve the economic situation in the country. Undoubtedly, Nyerere took to heart and possibly regretted his early retirement from the post of president. The elements of nostalgia for the era of Nyerere are still strong in Tanzanian society. Many Tanzanians believe that the years of Nyerere, despite all the difficulties, were happier and more abundant than now.

It should be borne in mind, however, that Nyerere was happy to see in his lifetime the full liberation of Africa from the yoke of colonialism, and in this respect his dream came true.

We bow our heads respectfully before the memory of this uncommon man and political figure, and we wish Tanzanian people well.

THE FATEFUL AUGUST OF 1968
HOT SUMMER IN DAR ES SALAAM
A Political Profile of Julius Kambarage Nyerere

Arkadi Glukhov

The summer in that year in Dar es Salaam had turned out to be especially hot and stuffy. Under the merciless scorching sun the city, since early morning, was gradually immersing itself in sultry lethargy, becoming by midday already sleepy and motionless. Now and then dark thunderclouds move in from the direction of the ocean, bringing with them heavy showers, which, however, did not bring any relief. The vapour from the scorched ground, asphalt, and roofs rose up, and it even became difficult to breathe because of the excessive humidity.

After the winter frosts of Moscow, and being sick with a heavy cold, a human organism hardly adapted to the tropical climate of East Africa. It has remained vividly in my memory that during the first weeks after my arrival I was permanently thirsty and invincibly lured by the Indian Ocean, which was only a few yards away from the windows of the first floor of the embassy building. It seemed that every member of the embassy's staff was obsessed with only one desire - to live to see the weekend, and to set off with their families on one of the many beaches, surrounding Dar es Salaam, for the whole day. On Saturdays and Sundays, the embassy became deserted with only one diplomat on duty and the security guards remaining at their posts. By evening, all had returned home tired but happy, despite of sunburn and the unavoidable bites of various insects. The swimmers had to be very careful not to stop on a sea-urchin, the wounds from which were very painful and which took long time to heal. The tsetse fly, carrier of a terrible disease, "sleeping sickness", a bane for local people and cattle in some regions, was also causing panic among the embassy personnel.

The rather small staff of the Soviet embassy worked harmoniously, in a quiet rhythm, without stress. Some of the diplomats were interested in observing the life of an exotic African country, and got acquainted with traditions and customs of the heterogeneous population consisting of over a hundred different ethnic groups, some of them still living inside a social structure close to primitive communalism. Naturally, the embassy centred its attention on domestic and foreign policies of the young state, the activities of its government and the ruling party, TANU, on the speeches and statements of the leader of the Tanzanian people, Julius Nyerere, who, at the time enjoyed huge popularity in the country.

Since the establishment of diplomatic relations between the two countries in 1961, Soviet-Tanzanian relations and cooperation had made progress in all directions. Moscow regarded Tanzania as a politically promising country, which had decided to purşue a course of socialist construction, and firmly adhered to a position of anti-imperialism.

The International Department of the CPSU Central Committee, which was in charge of practically all issues concerned with maintaining links and rendering assistance to the "fraternal" parties and revolutionary organisations, was especially satisfied with the ever growing political and ideological relationship between TANU and the CPSU, which was obviously backed by President Nyerere. His invariably friendly attitude to the Soviet diplomats, the spirit of mutual understanding and confidentiality that prevailed in contacts and conversations with him, helped the embassy staff to solve practical questions of cooperation between the two countries and parties, particularly in providing through Dar es Salaam Soviet assistance (including military) to the national liberation movements in South Africa, Mozambique, Southern Rhodesia and Namibia.

We observed with satisfaction that Nyerere showed an interest in the theory of Marxism-Leninism, the history of the USSR and Soviet experience in the construction of Socialism. It was known, that he regularly read the Soviet political literature and periodicals published in English, which his visitors had noticed on his bookshelves and on the desk in his study.

Moreover, from conversations with the president it became clear that he considers it important and useful for the Tanzanian public, TANU officials, and especially the youth to learn extensively about the life of the Soviet people and the "achievements of real socialism" in the USSR. He supported our offer to translate into Swahili, in an adapted form, some works of V.I. Lenin and speeches of the contemporary Soviet leaders. We were also delighted when we received not only his consent, but also his personal assistance in publishing the Dar es Salaam edition of the Soviet newspaper in Swahili *Urusi Leo* (Russia today), with the cooperation of the APN information bureau. The president also approved the organization of regular Moscow broadcasts to East Africa. In conversation with us, he gave us his advice as to what themes and topics would be most urgent and useful in these broadcasts. I remember that Nyerere in his address to the graduates of the TANU party school, "Kiwukoni College", specified the importance of using the experience of socialist transformation in the USSR, warning, however, against simply copying, and emphasizing the need to take into account specifically African conditions and local traditions.

President Nyerere's frequent contacts and conversations with the Soviet ambassador and various Soviet delegations visiting Dar es Salaam, were, as a rule, pithy and rich in content. His European education and high level of culture, breadth of views, and independent judgements - all this, combined with an irrepressible sense of humour, lambent wit, and his sheer personal charm, made Nyerere an extremely attractive and interesting person. At the same time, he was far from being a "simple" interlocutor. His deep knowledge in the field of world history and literature, international relations, and law required from his negotiators the appropriate knowledge, erudition, and a meaningful response. The diplomats in Dar es Salaam used to say jokingly that before going to talk to President Nyerere, it was necessary to thoroughly study Shakespeare, for the president had translated some of his works into Swahili.

However, let us return to the events of August 1968, when the "complete mutual understanding" and "good attitude" to us on the part of Nyerere, was quite unexpectedly, put to a hard test. The first disturbing symptoms, however, had already appeared in April and May, when Czechoslovakia was in the grip of Prague's reformers, who were fighting for "real democracy" and "socialism with a human face". These events were called the "Prague spring", and started to appear in the rather popular Tanzanian political lexicon. It became completely obvious, that the Tanzanian leadership and general public sympathized with Alexander Dubèek's people. Tanzanian mass media covered the events in Czechoslovakia in details, emphasizing that it was an attempt to oppose the "two socialisms", where the socialism of the "Soviet example" was already being looked at in a negative light. The "example" and "infallibility" of the Soviet Union and its "socialist experience" were on the wane in Tanzanian public opinion. The general public believed, not without good reason, that Moscow was putting obstacles in the way of Dubèek and his transformations, presenting itself as the conservative force. At that time, in conversations with Soviet diplomats Tanzanians frequently expressed bewilderment and disappointment with the position of the Soviet leaders.

All the controversy described above, caused serious anxiety in the Soviet embassy, which informed the Centre in some detail on the mood in Tanzanian society and its leadership. From Moscow we received instructions, which were standard in similar cases: "to strengthen elucidative work", "to expose Western propaganda", "to disclose before Tanzanians the underlying reason for the events in Czechoslovakia. And though the diplomatic staff were rather sceptical about such 'valuable instructions', nevertheless, they hoped that in due course everything would settle down. It seemed improbable, that the Soviet Union's prestige in Tanzania could be undermined in any way. However the subsequent events showed that these hopes proved to be false.

The unexpected intrusion of the Soviet troops into the territory of Czechoslovakia caused a wave of public indignation and protest in Dar es Salaam. On August 22-23, the Soviet embassy was virtually blocked by marchers and pickets. The police could hardly control protesters, especially of the students. Simultaneously crowds of the people were gathered at the Czechoslovakian embassy, expressing support and solidarity with Alexander Dubèek.

On August 24, Moscow had sent instruction to urgently visit President Nyerere and to inform him about "the difficult decision" made by the

Soviet Union and its allies under the Warsaw Treaty, and to explain him that the socialist countries, carrying out their "international duty", are acting "exclusively" in the interests of the people of Czechoslovakia and its "sound forces", which are menaced by an "international conspiracy" and an "imperialist aggression". The instruction ordered us to express hope for "understanding and support on the part of the president, government and people of Tanzania for which the people of the Soviet Union experience extremely friendly feelings".

The next day in the morning we went to see the president Julius Nyerere. The embassy was headed during this period by the Charge d'affaires G.Å. Samsonov. We heard the news over the car radio about clashes and first casualties in the streets of Prague, the arrest of Alexander Dubèek, the address of Ludwig Svoboda to the people, the underground extraordinary congress of the Communist Party of Czechoslovakia. At the entrance to the Presidential Palace we came across a "Tatra" car with the ambassador of Czechoslovakia in it. Some people on the pavement, having noticed a red flag on our car, started to shout and shake their fists at us. Our souls shrank in alarm.

President Nyerere met us in extremely official and cold way. He listened to the message of Samsonov in silence, and thanked him coldly. There then came an ominous pause. The president seemed unable to find suitable words for his response. It was not hard to guess that he was shocked by the Soviet Union's actions in Czechoslovakia and felt, probably, some difficulty in expressing an impartial opinion, within the framework of diplomatic courtesy. The further course of the meeting confirmed this.

Speaking more slowly than usual, and as though selecting his expressions with great care, Nyerere started by expressing sympathy with Samsonov, noting, that he had to carry out a difficult assignment from his government, proving the legitimacy of actions, which he himself did not consider legitimate. He went on to note that Tanzania believed firmly in strict observance of the UN Charter, in particular, its main principle: non-interference in the internal affairs of other states and respect for their sovereignty. He emphasized that this principle should be strictly observed by all states without exception, including great powers. He then recalled the principled position taken by Tanzania in connection with the American aggression in Vietnam. In conclusion, the president expressed his regret that he could not agree with the given explanations and reasons, in spite of all the respect and friendly attitude which the people of Tanzania feel for the Soviet Union.

Nyerere, visibly, with extreme self control contained his strong feelings on this issue. The president seemed to leave the conversation uncompleted. However, very soon it became obvious that he had found a way to finish it, and to say everything that he could not allow himself to say during the meeting with the Soviet diplomat.

The evidence of this is that two days after the memorable meeting, TANU's newspaper *The Nationalist* published an article under an intriguing heading "Pity the Ambassador", which immediately attracted the attention of the diplomatic corps and the paper's Tanzanian readership.

The article, written in excellent English, and in graceful literary style, was imbued with bitter irony and sarcasm. Hardly anyone was in doubt that its author was president Nyerere. A few days later, the Tanzanian ambassador to the USSR, Mr Mfinanga, in a confidential conversation confirmed Nyerere's authorship.

The author of this article wrote that it was a pity that the poor ambassador, who, carrying out the instructions of his government, must, for example, officially inform the leadership of the country where he is accredited, that the sun now rises not in the east, but in the west. The ambassador adduces reasons intended to justify intrusion of foreign troops into other country, calling this action the protection of socialism and democracy. As a clever man, the ambassador may be does not believe in these reasons himself, and it is even possible that he is ashamed for his country. It is quite obvious, that he, being an ambassador and a Soviet patriot, has no any choice, and he has to vindicate his government actions. We have only to sympathize with the dear ambassador, but we cannot agree with his reasons, as the sun still rises in the east, and sets in the west, and not the other way round. [16]

---

[16] See *The Nationalist* (Dar es Salaam), 26 August 1968

In the final part of the article, the irony and sarcasm concerning the ambassador disappears, giving place to a precise statement of the basic position of Tanzania on international affairs, which it firmly adheres to, be it Vietnam, Czechoslovakia or Southern Rhodesia. (In other words, be it the actions of the USA, USSR or Great Britain). Then, toward the end of the article, the author returns to his ironical tone and once again expresses sympathy with the "poor ambassador".

Thus, Nyerere, using the form of the newspaper feuilleton, publicly condemned the Soviet Union for its intrusion of Czechoslovakia. It is noteworthy that he made this condemnation without mentioning the Soviet Union "by name", so to say, and took as his target a top Soviet diplomat, with whom, despite of all irony, he, probably, sincerely sympathized.

Reflecting on these events, it becomes obvious that Nyerere, being a genuine democrat and honest-minded politician, could not act differently, i.e. to renege on his beliefs and principles. On the other hand, it was not so easy for Nyerere to do so, given his adherence to socialist ideals, and the high value he placed on good relations and friendship with the Soviet Union. It must also have been difficult for President Nyerere to stick to his principles at the cost of denting his, up till then, impeccable relations with the Soviet Union. The more so because Tanzania, as a "Frontline State", was in great need of Soviet aid and support, and received them.

In the subsequent (post 1968) years, the character of USSR-Tanzania relations and cooperation outwardly has not changed. Because of president Nyerere's diplomatic skills and honesty, as before, they were characterized as friendly and mutually advantageous for both parties. Tanzania continued to rate highly the role of the Soviet Union in the struggle against imperialism and colonialism, for world peace and international security, and for rendering assistance and support to the countries and peoples of Africa. However, it would be naive to believe, at the same time, that the events of 1968 connected with Czechoslovakia, have not left a negative impression of the Soviet Union in Tanzanian public opinion, and in the attitudes to the USSR held by country's ruling circle, and personally by president Nyerere himself. The former friendly attitude and confidentiality in our relationship was increasingly deteriorating into mere pragmatism.

Nyerere could hardly have been expected to surmise way back in 1968, that 20 years later, not in some remote backwater, but in the very Soviet Union itself, the socialist economic system would find itself in a deep crisis, and the leader of the party and the state Mikhail Gorbachev, would be proclaiming the necessity of "perestroika" (renovation) in all spheres, and would begin "reforming" socialism in the country. That is, he will begin to implement all the changes that two decades ago Alexander Dubèek had suggested, and which the Soviet Union did everything in its power, to stop him from making. Could Nyerere assume then, that the Soviet Union a "bulwark of world socialism" would suffer a crash as a "great socialist power", whose "wide experience", he, at one time, urged to be used in the construction of a new Tanzania? And, finally, could Nyerere foresee that in the heart of the "real" and "advanced socialism", the theory and practice of socialism would be subjected to the most severe criticism and actually eliminated from the life of the new state, now to be known as the Russian Federation?

Looking back at Nyerere's long-term political and state activity, one becomes convinced, that for the president of Tanzania socialism was not simply a propaganda term, or an element in political rhetoric in defining the way of development for his country. He also was far from using the concept of "socialism", for the sake of political benefit, to please Moscow or Beijing, as it had happened in some other countries of the Third World. By no means! Nyerere saw socialism in its "African variant" (the basic principles of which he had stated in the Arusha Declaration in 1967), above all, the optimal and speedy way of socio economic and political development for Tanzania, as well as for other African countries.

We may only guess what feelings overwhelmed this great democrat, outstanding statesman, and political figure of Africa, witnessing the collapse of socialism in the Soviet Union. Without doubt, for him it destroyed some of his hopes, and wreck of hopes, and wrecked some of his of illusions.

49

MY HAPPY MEMORY OF JULIUS NYERERE

Vladimir Aldoshin

My acquaintance with Africa started in Tanzania, where I worked from June 1974 to August 1978. Since then, much water has passed under the bridge, there were business trips and visits to other African states, but it was Tanzania with its lands, people and their leaders that has left the most bright and unforgettable imprints in my memory.

In the first after war years, the Moscow State Institute of International Relations did not train specialists for work on the "Black continent". There was no need for that. The situation changed sharply at the turn of the 1950s, when the world political map expanded with the addition of the new independent states of Africa. One obvious sign of these changes, and the new balance of forces on the international arena was that the UN General Assembly ceased to play the role of "the American voting machine". With the opening of new USSR embassies in Africa, the amount of work for Russian diplomats has increased considerably. To cope with the task, the Ministry of Foreign Affairs resorted to the transfer of some cadres from other locations, introducing a system of rotation.

Moscow has proceeded from the assumption that Tanzania adheres to realistic positions, consistently acts against neo-colonialism, and supports national liberation movements in Africa and beyond. This line corresponded with the views and activities of Julius Kambarage Nyerere, the first president of Tanzania and leader of TANU, the sole party on the Tanzanian mainland.

Nyerere was one of the authors of the Arusha Declaration of the 1967, which outlined the task of construction a socialist society in Tanzania. The author also set down the regulations in "The Leadership Code", was responsible for the concept of the creation of the *"Ujamaa"* villages, aimed at the reorganization of the traditional form of life of the rural population, and conceptualized the self-reliance policy for the country's development. It is worth noticing that neither in public statements, nor in personal conversations, did Nyerere use such terms as "socialist orientation", "African socialism" or similar concepts, believing that socialism as a social formation either does or does not exist.

My first meeting with president Nyerere took place in early summer of 1975 (summer by the northern hemisphere calendar), when I was chargè d'affaires of the USSR Embassy in Tanzania. The encounter took place in the president's private residence on the outskirts of Dar es Salaam, which served him also as a working study. It was a quiet, modest and cosy house with a green lawn and flowerbeds, facing the ocean and the coastal islands on the horizon. A minimum of guards and attendants, modesty in protocol requirements at public functions - in general were peculiar to Nyerere.

It took time and effort to prepare for the meeting, especially when it was to be a purposeful meeting with the head of state. It was necessary not only to clarify the position of my government, but also to envisage what complexities could happen at the first meeting that might disturb the establishment of a necessary working atmosphere. Whenever possible, it is advisable to secure support of the interlocutor, but also, to discuss the matter with him and, with due respect, to exert an allowable "pressure" on him. It was wise to define the form of the reference. To address him as "Mister" seemed too formal and, apparently, did not correspond to the spirit of relations between our countries. On the other hand, the word "comrade" sounded somewhat premature and a little unceremonious.

Within and outside Tanzania Nyerere usually was referred to as *Mwalimu* (the Teacher). It suited my interlocutor and, certainly, me. In such reference there was nothing deliberate or artificial. The point was not that Nyerere was highly educated intellectual, educational specialist, holder of English university diploma and *honoris causa* Ph.D. degrees, but rather that he had become a symbol of the long wished changes for the best.

The protocol practice has recorded many extraordinary occurrences, connected with the reference to the interlocutor, including at the highest level. During the official visit of the Chairman of the Presidium of the USSR Supreme Council, Nikolai Podgorny, in 1977, the parties had agreed to begin their speeches at the final state dinner with the words "Dear Comrade". Having received beforehand the text of Nyerere's speech, Podgorny learned that he was going to be addressed as "Mister" and immediately ordered the necessary change to be made to his own speech.

At dinner, Nyerere quietly has started to read his text beginning from words "Dear Comrade Chairman", and Podgorny imperturbably answered "Esteemed Mister President". It may be looked upon as a sort of triviality, a speechwriter's slip of the pen, a speechwriter being maybe unaware of the previous arrangement, but it gave rise to some nervousness amongst some people.

A few words about the subjects and the atmosphere of the conversations. In the seventies, connections between our countries and organizations were rather wide, and the positions on the important international questions, in our opinion, "coincided or were close". This was undoubtedly true concerning the support of the national liberation movements in the south of Africa. Moscow was interested also in Tanzanian support of the Soviet initiatives discussed in the UNO, and at other international meetings on disarmament, restriction of the arms race and other urgent questions of that time, as well as in attracting Tanzania to acknowledge their co-authorship of the appropriate resolutions.

Julius Nyerere was a positive and, I would say, talented interlocutor and he was also an attentive interested listener. This characteristic favourably distinguished him from other African leaders, I had to meet later. His desire to penetrate into the essence of the information was quite apparent, to understand ulterior motives behind it, and their possible consequences. As a rule, the Soviet offers met the benevolent reaction of the president of Tanzania. It couldn't be otherwise, as they were based on the so-called "common to all mankind values" and did not affect the political independence of Tanzania and its status as a non-aligned state. As far as I know, the same reaction was applied to our "antagonists", at the time, the USA and China.

It may be assumed that the benevolent attitude to those or other initiatives was not always translated in their support by Tanzanian diplomacy. Such was the case with the proposals on the direction to be taken, saved as a result of measures on disarmament, on the needs of the developing countries; about the proclamation of Africa as a nuclear weapon free zone, and about the proclamation of the Indian Ocean as a zone of peace, in the realization of which Tanzania was interested.

It is hardly necessary to track down any duality of such an approach, as it was often difficult to separate the propaganda from real components of some initiatives. The close association of Tanzania's positions with the Soviet political initiatives could have put in doubt the "non-aligned status" of the United Republic of Tanzania, and to give rise to discontent on the part of other countries, in cooperation with which Tanzania was interested for obvious reasons. In the USA Nyerere's "experiments" were regarded with an undertone of hostility, and predictions of failure.

Despite of dependence, first of all economic, on the West, and certain vacillations inherent in the non-aligned countries, Nyerere's line in both domestic and international policy was consistent and, as it was dubbed at the time, a "progressive" one. I believe that the real contribution of Tanzania, both political and material, and in particular, its assistance to the national liberation movement, is not properly appreciated yet. Suffice it to say, that the fact of opening and inclusion of the representation of the National Front of the Liberation of Southern Vietnam in the official list of diplomatic missions accredited in the country, issued by the Tanzanian foreign office, vividly reveals the attitude to the American intervention in Vietnam.

The human rights issue is also worth mentioning here. The year of 1975 marked an important stage of the Conference on Security and Cooperation in Europe, culminated by the signing of the Helsinki Final Act. The significance of this document goes far beyond the European continent and affects the interests of the developing countries. The opponents of the USSR actively used meetings on humanitarian questions for pressure on the Soviet delegation in a clause concerning human rights. Nyerere's position in these issues, stated in conversations and public speeches, was unequivocal and well-defined; among all human rights, important as they are, the most essential is the right to life, at any rate, in the developing countries.

Looking back through those years, I recollect that Nyerere never touched in his talks the concrete questions of Soviet-Tanzania economic relations, though they were rather extensive, and some of them as, for example, construction of a cement plant at Mbeya, a hydroelectric complex on the Kiwira River, and a gold mine at Chunya, were of great importance for the development of the southwest region of the country and caused a great deal of troubles both for the Soviets and Tanzanians. Nyerere usually entrusted such matters to his corresponding ministries and agencies. The cooperation in the military sphere developed more smoothly, though, shortly after the arrival, I learned with some surprise that Tanzanian servicemen on returning home after military training in the USSR had to go through political retraining, and only then were sent to their military units.

The USSR embassy in Tanzania worked as a whole in a quiet environment, the existing restrictions did not differ from those applied to other comparable embassies, and the treatment of Soviet employees was even and friendly.

From this, however, it does not follow that the Tanzanians closed their eyes to those events, which they assessed differently from the Soviet conceptions. The circulation of Soviet printed materials with the criticism of the Chinese State and Communist Party leaders' actions caused vigorous objections from Tanzania's side on the grounds that the latter does not tolerate its territory to be used for conducting an ideological struggle between the two, albeit also friendly, but foreign powers. In all fairness, it is necessary to note, that the same memoranda were also sent to the Chinese embassy concerning distribution of the anti-Soviet literature.

One morning, on opening the newspaper *The Daily News,* I came across the announcement that "a dangerous criminal" is wanted. In the attached photo, I recognised one of our Soviet journalists. On my memorandum and request as to "why it was not possible to settle the matter through the usual channels", the Ministry of Foreign Affairs answered that the ministry was not concerned. I do not think that similar incidents, taking into account the character and essence of our interstate relations, could happen without the consent and approval of the president. I am not prepared to consider them as some kind of "anti-actions", and I believe that that was a reminder to us about the sovereignty and independence of their state.

My desire to visit one of the *Ujamaa* villages was not accepted. It seemed to me that the good working relations, which had been established between the chief of protocol and me, would ensure that there would be no objection of my visiting such a village. The point is that it was the foreign office that had suggested and organized my trip to Dodoma, had arranged meetings with Tanzanian and foreign experts, a visit to the building sites, and nurseries of decorative plants, and even the site, where the USSR embassy was to be built.

The truth is that the economic councillor and I had to state in our report to the Centre our opinion that the transfer of the capital was a matter for the distant future. And the chance to see *Ujamaa* in action did not happen, as, according to the chief of protocol, the suitable village was too far from Dar es Salaam. Probably, under existing circumstances at that time, such a trip by a foreign diplomat, although he was representative of a friendly state, was undesirable.

These are some of my impressions collected and kept of Tanzania and its first president Julius Kambarage Nyerere, statesman and philosopher, dreamer and practical man, indisputable leader of his country and people, who, looking from to-day's position maybe was ahead of his time.

After Tanzania, I had a chance to meet other leaders of the countries of Tropical Africa, but they were people of other dimension, not reaching that national and Pan-African level, which was achieved by Julius K. Nyerere.

MWALIMU JULIUS KAMBARAGE NYERERE
(1922-1999) TEACHER, POLITICIAN, POET

Vladimir Ovchinnikov

Мечты Господни многооки,
Рука Дающего щедра,
И есть еще, как он, пророки,
Святые рыцари добра.
Н. Гумилев. Пророки

[The Lord's dreams are unbounded,
The giving Hand is lavish,
And there are still prophets like Him,
The holy kindhearted knights.]
Nikolai Gumilyov. *The Prophets.*

Dear colleagues, in my opinion, it is important today that, thanks to the Institute for African Studies of the Russian Academy of Sciences we have assembled in this hall to pay homage to Mwalimu Julius Kambarage Nyerere, a famous son of Africa. Mwalimu was a true Catholic and regular churchgoer. He repeatedly met the Popes, both in Africa and in the Vatican. Moreover, in the last years of his life, his friends even nicknamed him an "African Evangelist" for his poetic translation into Swahili of some Gospels of the New Testament. Unfortunately, at the moment, these translations are out of my reach. I share the opinions stated here that the life and activity of Mwalimu Julius Kambarage Nyerere made a big contribution to an epoch in the history not only of Tanzania, East Africa and Africa as a whole, but also to the history of the world during the second half of the 20th century.

I shall confine my remarks today to brief theses about Mwalimu's positive contribution to the development of education and culture of the United Republic of Tanzania. I shall try to explain my own feelings about this outstanding African figure.

I, as an interpreter of the Swahili language, was lucky enough to get acquainted with Mwalimu in 1965 and to meet him during official negotiations both in Tanzania and here in Russia. As a matter of fact, he became my informal teacher, not only helping me to become aware of the riches and subtleties of the Swahili language, but also of the culture, customs and manners of the peoples of Tanzania and East Africa. He was surprisingly warm with interpreters, giving them their due for their hard work. His phenomenal visual memory always amazed me. He could recommend certain history books, or books concerned with the Swahili language to an interpreter and then, after a long while, when he met this same person again, he would ask about his recommended books, and how valuable his advice had been. And I know for sure that he met and gave kind pieces of advice not only to me, but also to dozens of other interpreters.

It is always interesting to know how the personality of such an individual as Nyerere was formed, and what the background to his life course was.

Kambarage Nyerere, the 26th child in a large African family, was born on April 13th, 1922 in a small village on the shores of one of the world largest body of fresh water, Lake Victoria, approximately 40 kilometres east of the town of Musoma in northern Tanganyika, then a League of Nations Trusteeship Territory under British administration.

Kambarage's father, Nyerere Burito, was Chief of the Zanaki, a small but significant pastoral tribe in the Mara region. Chief Nyerere Burito died in 1942, at the age of eighty-two. Kambarage's mother, "Bibi" (Madam), as he affectionately named her, Christina Mgaya Wang'ombe, was the 5th among 18 wives of Nyerere Burito. She lived to a great age, and always followed with interest and prides her son's career. She died in 1997 at the age of over 100 years. The death of his mother hit Nyerere hard.

According to the tradition of all the pastoral peoples of Africa, children at an early age do what they can to help their parents look after their animals. The young Kambarage was no. Until he was twelve years old, he helped to graze the cattle of his father. However, his big brother Edward and some village elders noticed the young herd boy's lively mind. They persuaded Chief Nyerere Burito to send his son to Mwisenge Primary Boarding School in Musoma town. Kambarage was baptized and chose Julius as his Christian name, probably, in honour of Julius Caesar, who has become an idol for him.

The newly converted Julius successfully passed his final primary exams, and was admitted at the exclusive elite Tabora School for boys from the "royal" families of Tanganyika. It was at this school where Nyerere made the acquaintance of many of his future colleagues, and where he first showed his talent for leadership. All through his life, he has been known as a steadfast fighter for justice, equality and humanism.

After study at Tabora School, Julius entered Makerere University College in Uganda, then a citadel of higher education for all the countries of British East Africa: Kenya, Tanganyika, Uganda, and Zanzibar. In 1945, having received at Makerere a Diploma in Education, he became a teacher at St. Mary's Secondary School in Tabora. After four years of teaching, the school management recommended young Julius for study at Edinburgh University in Scotland. He became the first Tanganyikan to be admitted to this higher educational institution and the first Tanganyikan to receive a Master of Arts degree. During his tears in Scotland, he studied with enthusiasm the history of the Roman Empire, established close contacts with the Fabian Socialist Society, and became a staunch advocate of a socialist reorganization of society.

In 1952 Nyerere returned home and was appointed a teacher at St. Francis College, Pugu, then a missionary educational institution, a few kilometres southwest of Dar es Salaam. Nowadays it is a government institution, and is known as Pugu Secondary School. It was here that a young and vigorous teacher plunged into cultural and religious environment, a deeply Islamised traditional Swahili society. Just in public pronouncements, addressing mainly the Muslim leaders of Tanganyika African Association (TAA) Nyerere perfected his oratorical and poetic skill in classical Swahili language. And it is quite natural that he received the honourable nickname Mwalimu (Teacher), which became a component part of his name. And nowadays any Tanzanian immediately will answer to your question, who is Mwalimu. During the same years he has brilliantly mastered the Swahili game 'Bao' (a kind of a Persian game backgammon) Mwalimu said jokingly that the mastering of the Swahili prosody and the 'Bao' game he considered the most effective weapon in the struggle for independence.

These were the years, when Mwalimu reached the level of national leader by becoming the first President of the Tanganyika African National Union (TANU), created in 1954, and which led Tanganyika to independence in December 1961. For his contribution to the struggle for independence of the native land, Mwalimu received one more honourable name, "Baba wa Taifa" (Father of Nation). In 1985, after 24 years of the faithful service as the head of state, Mwalimu voluntarily left the presidential office.

As a teacher, statesman, and political figure Mwalimu made an invaluable personal contribution to the development of education and Swahili-language literature. In public pronouncements he constantly emphasized that a country without its culture is just a crowd of people, deprived of the spirit, capable to forge them into a nation. As far back as in 1958, at the heat of struggle for independence, Mwalimu, first among the leaders of East Africa, declared, "We, the people of Tanganyika, would like to light a torch and install it on the top of Mountain Kilimanjaro so that it will shine beyond our borders and bring hope where there is despair, love where there is hate and dignity where there is humiliation"[17]. Soon these words were turned into a popular song, which inspired the vast masses on the struggle for the honour and dignity all over East and Central Africa, where the Swahili language is widespread.

Mwalimu, a universally recognized Malenga (poet-narrator of folk tales), was closely associated with the outstanding figures of Swahili literature: Shaaban Robert, Amri Abedi, S.A. Kandoro, and others. He maintained a correspondence with them in verses, in which the essential questions of life were reflected. In my opinion, the strongest influence on Mwalimu Malenga was exerted by the literature of the most esteemed poet Muyaka bin Haji al-Ghassaniy (1776-1840), who was named a master of qvatrian verses, classic of Swahili versification, "a father of the Swahili poetry". Muyaka wrote the following of those ready to lay their lives in the battle for freedom (in Kiswahili):

---

[17] See Dar es Salaam Guede. 1999, No 16, p. 16

Simba wa Maji
Ndimi tazo nembetele, majini ndimi mbuaji
Nishikapo nishikile, nyama ndimi mshikaji
Ndipo nami wasinile, nimewashinda walaji
Kiwiji simba wa maji, msonijua juani!
Maji yakijaa tele, huandama maleleji
Pepo za nyuma na mbele, hawinda wangu windaji
Huzamia maji male male yasofika mbiji
Hiwiji simba wa maji, msonijua juani.[18]

In the heydays of the 'Ujamaa' theory (Tanzanian brand of socialism), apparently under the influence of Muyaka, Mwalimu wrote a poem, "The ship of a nation" which begins by the words, "In high seas one cannot do without a helmsman".

At any opportunity Mwalimu invariably came back to his main postulate, "Swahili is a very euphonic and well-grounded language, however, only its effective use is capable to promote even greater growth of its euphony and depth". It was Mwalimu who did his best to proclaim Swahili the official national language, at first in Tanganyika (1962), and then in Tanzania (1964). He was a man who coupled acts with words. Having a perfect command of English, he was convinced that neither the nation, nor culture could exist without a native language; and it was Swahili that was capable to carry out such predestination. In addition, he made his practical contribution to realize this idea.

He began with the translation of Shakespeare's 'Julius Caesar'. In the foreword to a masterpiece of the English and world literature, issued in 1963 in Swahili, Mwalimu wrote how he began the translation process. In translating this piece of work he did not imagine what would happen to it. First, he did not assume that he would translate the entire book. Secondly, he did not assume publishing of the translation. His purpose was to find such an occupation, which would allow him to distract himself from an exhaustive daily routine. However, as the translation ardour grew, his desire to accomplish the work rose up as well. Then

---

[18] Mulika No. 10, Chuo cha Uchunguzi wa Lugha ya Kiswahili Chuo Kikuu, Dar es Salaam, March, 1977, uk. 5.

some of his friends, by learning about his enthusiasm, began to urge him to consummate the work and to agree to publish the translation.[19] The same foreword gives a thorough analysis of distinguishing features of versification in English and Swahili, reveals the "secrets" of a creative approach to the vocabulary and emotionality of the exposition. After the Swahili translation of 'Julius Caezar' was published, it became an important tutorial for teachers of higher and secondary schools not only in Tanzania, but also at the universities of the advanced countries of the world: Great Britain, France, Germany, USA, Japan, Australia, and Canada etc., where Swahili was taught. Then followed new translations on Swahili of Shakespeare's works: *Mackbeth* and *Merchants of Venice*.

The translations, performed by Mwalimu, promoted the strengthening and development of national language, as well as the development of philosophical and political terminology. And finally, it found its reflection in The Chama Cha Mapinduzi (CCM: Revolutionary Party) Programme for 1987-2002 and in other party policy documents prepared under the guidance of Mwalimu. CCM remains the ruling party in Tanzania, though the former objectives and programmes were replaced with the new ones, which took into account the present-day situation in Tanzania and beyond. Even so, the former terminology was preserved and was widely applied in mass media both in Tanzania, and at the foreign centres of information and African studies.

It is apt to add, that any public pronouncement of Mwalimu was well thought-out, and it could be taken as a paradigm of the modern Swahili language, as a graceful miniature, in which there are its own dramatic personae. Unfortunately, on certain parameters many of the present leaders of Kenya and Tanzania, with I had a chance to get acquainted, did not go in any comparison with Mwalimu's oratorical art. And, as I presume, this is caused by the lack of diligence in preparation of their speeches in Swahili, which was inherent to Mwalimu.

To sum up, I would like to express our common deep sorrow at the death

---

[19] See Shakespeare W., Julius Caezar. Mfasiri Julius K. Nyerere. Nairobi, 1963, p

of Julius Kambarage Nyerere, which occurred on 14 October 1999, at the St. Thomas Hospital in London. He left this world and his numerous worshippers. We are firmly convinced that in the field of national education and culture Mwalimu managed to erect to himself and to leave to his posterity and admirers of his creative work "a monument not made by hands". And the people's path to it will never overgrow with grass the Swahili literature and its creators are alive. And in addition, it would be very desirable to believe and to hope that for the kind terrestrial deeds Mwalimu, as the true Christian, could deserve at the Most High the award in the Heaven...

Asanteni Sana – Thank you very much for your attention.

REMINISCENCES OF SOME MEETINGS
WITH JULIUS NYERERE

Vladimir Shubin

The people who took floor here were acquainted with Julius Nyerere for a long time. I am in another situation, though for the first time I met or, more precisely, for the first time have seen Nyerere more than 35 years back, in 1964, in Cairo, during the second OAU Assembly of Heads of State and Government. The African leaders, Gamal Abdel Nasser's guests, were passing along Cairo streets in open cars, and thousands of Egyptians welcomed them.

Quarter of century later, during our last meeting, Nyerere recollected the importance of this assembly, which had adopted a resolution on the inviolability of borders of the African countries that have been left from colonial times, and on preservation of their integrity. Though this decision was exposed to criticism in various quarters, it saved Africa from the numerous conflicts. In fact, the only case, when one part of a state was allowed to separate, was the recognition of independence of Eritrea.

Conversely, the example of Tanzania, a country with more then 100 ethnic groups, and which managed to forge a uniform nation, proved the wisdom of Nyerere and his colleagues shown by them in 1964. Indeed, the stability is a distinctive feature of Tanzania. It makes the country a unique nation on the African continent, and favourably distinguishes it from other states of the world. Very largely, this stability is based on an uniting factor, the Swahili language, which Nyerere valued and cherished. The stability of the country is also attributed to Mwalimu's efforts on providing for the access to education, public health services and satisfaction of other basic needs of all population of the country, and not just a narrow circle of the privileged class.

The achievements of Tanzania in the social sphere and the maintenance of its stability were recognised even by those who criticized the Nyerere's domestic policy.

At the international plan, the authority of Nyerere was recognised in the South, West, and East. He was a *Honoris Causa* Doctor of a number of universities, the International Lenin Peace Prize winner. It does not mean that his foreign policy satisfied everybody. On the contrary, his criticism of the West powers for their cooperation with the apartheid regime, no less than of the Soviet intervention in Czechoslovakia, and then in Afghanistan, was based on firm moral principles. It is necessary to admit that his independent line was not always understood and accepted in our country.

Ambassador Vyacheslav Ustinov mentioned here that Leonid Brezhnev on "technical reasons" could not meet Julius Nyerere during his State visit to Moscow, almost 30 years ago. God grant, the matter was really "technical". But Gorbachev, whose actions Nyerere (as well as many others) originally welcomed and supported, could not find time to receive him, despite the fact that Nyerere, leaving the presidency, not only retained his position as the Chairman of the ruling CCM Party, but, it is safe to say, that he represented the "South" as a whole in the relations with the "West" and "East".

My colleagues mentioned here Nyerere's positions on the Soviet invasion of Czechoslovakia in 1968. Yes, there was a Czechoslovakia, but there was also a Biafra, which was recognised by Tanzania as an independent state, contrary to the course of the OAU. The Soviet Union refused to recognise Biafra, and this issue also caused serious problems in our bilateral relations.

In any case, the contribution of Nyerere in the achievement of the independence by the peoples of Southern Africa and in the strengthening of the peace on the African continent cannot be overlooked. Under his guidance Tanzania became a vital base country, practically, for all liberation movements in Southern Africa. It also became the home for thousands of freedom fighters, an asylum, where they could find their friends and allies. I had a chance to visit Dar es Salaam for the first time in 1967, providing the transportation of the FRELIMO cadres for training in the Soviet Union. Later, there were other visits: for participation in the CCM congress in 1982 and in the conference on Southern Africa in Arusha in 1984.

But most unforgettable were my two trips, in December 1997 and in June 1999.

The first one was connected with the participation in a conference titled: Reflections on African Leadership: 40 Years After Independence, which, though not formally, was devoted to Nyerere's 75th birthday anniversary. It gave me an opportunity to be convinced of Nyerere's high human qualities and of his magnanimity. In the report devoted to the late President of the African National Congress of South Africa, Oliver Tambo, and, in particular, to his relations with Nyerere, I also tried to open some of the little-known pages of history. One of them is connected to closing upon the decision by the Tanzanian leadership of an ANC camp in Kongwa, in 1969, that has resulted in the 'exodus' from Tanzania of the 'Umkonto we Sizwe' fighters, basically to the Soviet Union. Naturally, I experienced some awkwardness, when I learned that I should read the report at the presence of Nyerere, sitting in the first row, and, more so, when he took the floor to comment on my message.

However, my fears were vain. With a sense of humour, inherent in him, Nyerere admitted that he had convinced in due time the leader of the Zimbabwe African People's Union (ZAPU), Joshua Nkomo, to leave Dar es Salaam for home ('and he was thrown for ten years in prison'), he also had convinced the President of SWAPO, Sam Nujoma, to leave our country (then I, probably, thought more about Tanzania, than about Namibia'), but "I did not remember, whether it was made in the relation to the ANC". "But if I have done so, then I was wrong", he added, and it was a load off my mind.

That day Mwalimu continued the conversation with me, but entirely on other questions. Being the Head of the Centre of the South, he was interested in the data, cited by me, on the character of economic relations of Russia with the West. In my presentation I tried to show that Russia and other former Soviet republics are far from being rivals to the developing countries, rather, both are the victims of a plunder of their natural resources, and that "in an exchange" per each dollar received from the West as the credits or the investments, Russia was losing five, or maybe even ten, dollars in a form of the capital flight.

Our discussion on this question was continued a year and a half later, when Professor Haroub Othman of Dar es Salaam University and I were visitors to Mwalimu's native village Butiama in northwest Tanzania. The trip from the centre of the same province Mwanza to Butiama deserves a separate story (it took us seven hours to overcome the distance about 200 kilometres long, since it was necessary to repair our motor vehicle seven times. Haroub asked me, "is the magazine *Ogonyok* yet alive? So you would venture to write an article about our trip". We arrived in the evening, and the conversation with Nyerere took place the next day. The talk was short, but it was followed with a long dinner, during which we discussed many questions: from the aggression of NATO against Yugoslavia ('absolutely illegal war', such was Nyerere's judgement) up to the necessity of resistance to dictatorship by one 'superpower' and international financial institutions. Mwalimu was interested also in the reasons of the Soviet Union's collapse, and about the present situation in Russia. I remember Nyerere saying that in the 1986 Party Congress Gorbachev has made a deep analysis of the situation in the country, but he turned off the chosen road.

This meeting with Mwalimu was fruitful in one more respect. Professor Othman confessed to me later that he has spent almost seven years of futile attempts to urge Nyerere to start writing his memoirs and finally has succeeded. "Earlier I refused" said Nyerere to me, "but now I think that the time has come to start this work. The doctors advise me to lower the activity, but I hope to accomplish my mission of the intermediary in Burundi by the end of this year and then I shall be glad to accept here, in Butiama, the Tanzanian historians, which will help me in this new venture'.

Seeing us off and bidding me farewell near his old house, Mwalimu has noticed:"The Army have constructed for me the new house, too large. I do not hurry to move in. At first, it is necessary to transfer there my library, but now I shall have the space to host the visitors" Then he asked me, when I should come to Tanzania again. I was sure, that we should meet again, maybe, at the future presentation of his memoirs. Mwalimu looked much younger of his 77 years, and nothing threatened that it had been our last meeting.

JULIUS NYERERE HAS APPROVED OF
A MULTI-PARTY SYSTEM IN TANZANIA IN THE 1990s.

Lubov Prokopenko

In the new international environment caused, first of all, by the collapse of socialism in East Europe and disintegration of the USSR, as well as the establishment of multi-party systems in a number of tropical African countries, the leaders of Tanzania were necessitated to carry out political reforms. To no small degree this also was promoted by the pressure of the West, as its aid in supporting structural adjustment programs (or programs of economic revival, as they were called in Tanzania) were conditioned on the implementation of liberal political reforms. However, the negative aftermaths of these programs, deepening of the social inequality, plundering of the state-owned property, instead of its privatisation, pervasive corruption, became a serious threat to the country's stability.

In June 1990, Tanzania experienced heated discussions on the problem of feasibility to transfer to the multi-party system. Julius Nyerere stated that the CCM did not aspire to hegemony. The key African politician, a long-time advocate of a one-party system, has turned out to be a promoter of political pluralism.

In August 1990, Ali Hassan Mwinyi was elected the chairman of the CCM. In 1991, a special Commission on the multi-party system was set up. The Commission advanced the main argument in favour of the multi-party system; the necessity to obviate obstacles in the way to democracy, for one party system is incompatible with democratic processes. The Commission especially emphasized the necessity of a prohibition on creation of political parties on religious, ethnic or racial basis.

In February 1992, CCM announced that the one-party system had ceased to exist, and the registration of new political parties was allowed. In a short space of time a lot of opposition parties were formed. They required the prompt realization of the constitutional reform and introduction of the multi-party system.

By condemning the trend for excessive proliferation of the parties (by mid-1992 there were a dozen of them), Nyerere opted for two- or three-party system, believing that such an arrangement would be self-sufficient and would promote the creation of a new effective and democratic mechanism. He expected that a healthy competition would put an end to the obvious political stagnation of the CCM. The anxiety on the preservation of the Party's prestige among the population has motivated Nyerere to remind to the incumbent authorities of the necessity to avoid eulogy of the leaders, empty rhetoric, unjustified secrecy and protectionism.

On October 29 1995, Tanzania held the first in its history general elections on a multi-party basis. The CCM won an absolute majority of seats in the parliament. Benjamin Mkapa was elected the President of the Republic.

The process of liberalization of political relations in Tanzania is in the making. The five-year interval of time, since the country has returned to the multi-party system, naturally, does not allow offering comprehensive conclusions and generalizations. It is only the first step in the process of political and social changes. For Tanzania, as well as for other African states, democratisation is a long process fraught with risks and difficulties, because of the backwardness of socio economic and political structures of the African society, the absence of strong democratic traditions, and low level of political culture.

These problems are common to all African states embarked on a path of political reforms. The issue is the growing disillusionment and political apathy of the masses. The abandonment of socialism (be it an 'African socialism' or 'Ujamaa') left many poor people without a goal. As a political scientist, Patrick Ollawa, wrote in the distant 70s, "...It should be evident that such a goal cannot be attained without providing the masses with the opportunities for *meaningful participation* in the process" [20]

---

[20] Ollawa, Patrick E. *Participatory Democracy in Zambia. The Political Economy of National Development.* Arthur H. Stockwell Ltd. Dewon. 1979, p. 478

CONTRIBUTORS

Vladimir Aldoshin, Ambassador Extraordinary and Plenipotentiary of the RF, Counsellor of the Soviet Embassy in Tanzania in 1974-1978.

Arkadi Glukhov, PhD (Hist.), Ambassador Extraordinary and Plenipotentiary of the RF, Counsellor of the Soviet Embassy in Tanzania in1968-1974.

Nikolai Kosukhin, Dr Sc. (Hist.), Professor, Leading Research Fellow of the RAS Institute for African Studies.

Eva Lilian Nzaro, Ambassador Extraordinary and Plenipotentiary of the United Republic of Tanzania to the Russian Federation.

Vladimir Ovchinnikov, PhD (Hist.), Senior Research Fellow of the RAS Institute of General History.

Lubov Prokopenko, PhD (Hist.), Secretary of the RAS Academic Council for the Problems of Africa

Svetlana Shlyonskaya, Research Fellow of the RAS Institute for African Studies.

Vladimir Shubin, Dr Sc. (Hist.), Deputy Director of the RAS Institute for African Studies.

Vassili Solodovnikov, Dr Sc. (Econ.), Corresponding Member of the RAS, Ambassador Extraordinary and Plenipotentiary of the RF, Principal Research Fellow of the RAS Institute for African Studies.

Vyacheslav Ustinov, Ambassador Extraordinary and Plenipotentiary of the RF, Counsellor of the Soviet Embassy in Tanzania in 1962-1966, Ambassador of the USSR to Tanzania in 1969-1972.

Yuriy Vinokurov, PhD (Hist.), Head of the Centre for Tropical Africa Studies of the RAS Institute for African Studies.

Christopher Elkington, B.A. Cambridge, formerly of the Institute of Development Studies, University of Dar es Salaam. Editor of the English language translation.

SUMMARY

This is a collection of papers contributed to the Julius Nyerere Memorial Conference held in Moscow at the RAS Institute for African Studies in January 2000. Among the contributors are scholars, public figures and policy-makers.

In the opening speech, Professor Alexei Vassiliev, Director of the Institute for African Studies, emphasized Julius Nyerere's significant role in the history of the African Continent and of the whole world, which still waits to be fully recognized.

Eva Nzaro, Tanzania's Ambassador to Russia, highlighted the outstanding contribution of Mwalimu Julius Nyerere to the liberation of Africa from colonialism and to the development of Tanzania as an independent state, which provides peaceful and decent life to over 100 ethnic groups.

In the report about Nyerere's life, Professor Nikolai Kosukhin underlined the role of the first president of Tanzania as a great politician and philosopher theorist.

The papers of Russian diplomats, Vyacheslav Ustinov, Vassili Solodovnikov, Vladimir Aldoshin, Arkadi Glukhov, and the Institute's Deputy Director Vladimir Shubin, contain their recollections of meetings with Julius Nyerere.

Russian researchers Lyubov Prokopenko and Vladimir Ovchinnikov in their papers analyse Julius Nyerere's activity as the founder and leader of the TANU party and his linguistic works.

Printed in the United Kingdom
by Lightning Source UK Ltd.
120505UK00001B/4